D0870210

Mary of Nazareth

Mary of Nazareth

FEDERICO SUAREZ

 Scepter

Originally published with the title *Our Lady the Virgin*.
Copyright © 1956 Federico Suarez

Nihil obstat:
  Aloysius C. Kemper, S.J., Censor Theol. Deputatis

Imprimatur:
  + Albert G. Meyer, Archbishop of Chicago
  November 21, 1958

Second Edition
Copyright © 2003 Scepter Publishers, Inc., New York
www.scepterpublishers.org

CONTENTS

INTRODUCTION

The Virgin Mary is the most perfect creature who ever came from the hands of God. She is so good, so simple, so delicate, so extraordinarily humble and pure that one cannot help loving her.

Her stay in the world was hardly noticed by her contemporaries. It is the same with our own lives; there is nothing extraordinary, nothing that attracts attention. But in the eyes of God, the Virgin Mary was unique, and her part in creation was indispensable. The Father gave her to us, she gave us the Son, and she gave herself to the Holy Spirit. She gladdens the hearts of her children because she is so loving and has such a maternal heart.

Like the Virgin, however, we also mean something to God, and we have our little part to play in the universe, and each of us in a certain sense is indispensable; each of us is unique.

And perhaps the thought of our Mother in heaven and her life on earth may help us to emulate her and try to be what she was, the most cooperative of God's creatures that has ever existed. We must always keep in mind the fact that our life, if it has any purpose at all, derives this purpose from God and from the small part we have to play in creation, the purpose for which we have been created and appropriately gifted.

We know little, it is true, about the life of our Lady, but really it is not necessary to know much more. Full of grace from the first instant of her conception, the life of the Virgin Mary is both unique and exemplary. It is true that there is no other model than Jesus Christ, but it is also true that there has never been any other creature who imitated him so faithfully and who so exactly reproduced the image of her Son. And if God did not want to give us the Word directly, but by means of the Virgin, surely the best way to imitate Christ is to imitate our Lady.

I

THE ANNUNCIATION

In the sixth month the angel Gabriel was sent from God to a city of Galilee named Nazareth, to a virgin betrothed to a man whose name was Joseph, of the house of David; and the virgin's name was Mary. And he came to her and said, "Hail, full of grace, the Lord is with you!" But she was greatly troubled at the saying, and considered in her mind what sort of greeting this might be. And the angel said to her, "Do not be afraid, Mary, for you have found favor with God. And behold, you will conceive in your womb and bear a son, and you shall call his name Jesus. He will be great, and will be called the Son of the Most High; and the Lord God will give to him the throne of his father David, and he will reign over the house of Jacob for ever; and of his kingdom there will be no end." And Mary said to the angel, "How can this be, since I have no husband?" And the angel said to her, "The Holy Spirit will come upon you, and the power of the Most High will overshadow you; therefore the child to be born will be called holy, the Son of God. And, behold, your kinswoman Elizabeth in her old age has also conceived a son; and this is the sixth month with her who was called barren. For with God nothing will be impossible." And Mary said, "Behold, I am the handmaid of the Lord; let it be to me according to your word." And the angel departed from her.

LUKE 1: 26–38

The fact and its significance

The scene could not be simpler, nor could it be related more simply. A virgin named Mary was in her house in Nazareth.

9

She was young, hardly an adolescent—tradition says that she was about fourteen or fifteen years old—and she was espoused to a man named Joseph, of the house of David.

One day, perhaps when she is at prayer, as painters and spiritual writers like to represent her, she suddenly realizes that she is not alone. An angel has entered, and he greets her with such unexpected words that the Virgin is momentarily disconcerted. The words catch her completely unawares. Her first reaction to the angel's greeting is a completely natural one; she is confused. But she is not so confused as to be dumbfounded, or to lose her presence of mind. On the contrary she begins to think what such words could mean, addressed to her, to her precisely, such praise, especially from the mouth of an angel. What might be the explanation of such an occurrence?

Gabriel, the angel, hastens to calm her by clarifying the mystery: she is going to conceive in her womb, to give birth to a Son whom she shall call Jesus; this Son will be great, and he will be called the Son of the Most High, and God will give him the throne of David, in order that he may reign eternally in the house of Jacob, and his reign shall have no end.

The Virgin Mary, like all Israelites of her time, was well versed in the Scriptures. From her earliest childhood she had been instructed in the revelations according to the customs of the Jews; and the marvelous history of her people—the chosen people—was known to her in all its implications. She knew that the prophecies would be fulfilled in the coming of a Savior who would redeem Israel from its sins. The idea of a Messiah, as well as the passages of Scripture which spoke of him and the messianic prophecies and phrases which referred to him, were all familiar to her.

The words of the angel sounded like a prophecy to her; and not only because of the words he used, but also because of her extraordinary and interior sensitivity to the mysterious voice of God, she realized clearly that Gabriel was unfolding to her the Creator's plan for her: she was to become the Mother of the Messiah, of the Redeemer. She was to be that virgin who was spoken of by the prophet Isaiah, virgin who would conceive and give birth to a son w would be Emmanuel, that is to say, God with us (Is 7:14, But how was this going to happen?

This was precisely the question that the angel Gabriel aroused in Mary, the only question. The news of the messenger is already understood and is absolutely clear; it allows no room for conjecture or confusion. But she is a virgin and, furthermore, as a child she offered her virginity to God, pledging herself completely to God alone. If a virgin is to conceive, and she is that Virgin, how is this to be, "since I have no husband?"

It is impossible to interpret Mary's question as a hidden or veiled, but firm, determination to preserve her virginity even at the price of not being the Mother of the Messiah. It is inconceivable that she could put anything above the divine will, above God's plan for her, even if it was something of such high value and so pleasing to God as her virginity. If she had put her virginity first, she would have been putting her own will before the explicit will of God. That would imply a sin of pride and this is impossible because she was full of grace.

The statement "I have no husband" was her way of conveying to the angel that she had given herself to God. This giving of herself had not been the effect of capriciousness but of an impulse of the Holy Spirit, of God himself. But now God, through Gabriel, was telling her that she was going to conceive and be a mother. How could this be? She was not concerned about the apparent contradiction between the two signs from God; she knew that God could not contradict himself; perhaps she was concerned because she did not know precisely what part she was to play, what she herself was to do. She simply asked for clarification; for in order to participate fully in the divine plan, she needed a clear knowledge of how she was to act, a clear idea of the part she was to play.

And again the angel explains to her that this is not to be the work of any man but the work of God himself; for the Holy Spirit will overshadow her, and make her conceive.

that no

son will be called the Son of God: God's

need for any more explanation, but
verpowering, so inconceivable to any
far from all natural laws and all human
that Gabriel gave her a sign: Elizabeth, her
no was old and sterile, had conceived and was in
sixth month, for nothing shall be impossible with God.
Nothing, not even that a virgin, without losing her virginity,
should be a mother, not even that God should be a Father, a
Son, and a Spouse.

The Virgin Mary gives her answer immediately: *Fiat*,
"Thy will be done." She does not ask for time to think it
over; she has not the slightest doubt or hesitation. She understood immediately, according as Gabriel spoke his message, what God wanted of her; she asks a question, a very
intelligent question, in order to learn exactly, not what God
wants of her, which she already knows, but exactly how his
will is to be accomplished. And as soon as she understands,
she gives herself entirely to the will of her Creator.

Immediately the Word became flesh. The Son of God,
the Second Person of the Trinity, was conceived in the virgin
womb of Mary. And this, the most astounding and admirable
occurrence in the universe since the world began, since
the creation of the cosmos out of nothing, was brought
about with the greatest simplicity and in the most absolute
privacy, without any spectacle, without any fanfare or publicity, without anyone knowing it.

* * *

In the light of this singular event which occurred so
quickly in a humble little house in Nazareth, and examining all the facts together, one discovers first of all that for
the Virgin Mary this event was the major turning point in
her entire life. Until then her life had been lived in quiet
obscurity, and suddenly this most extraordinary event (that
is, an event outside the ordinary) places her in the limelight. This sudden moment of illumination was the culmi-

nating moment of her entire life, a moment in which she suddenly realized the reason for her existence, the reason for everything.

By the Annunciation, the Virgin clearly understood that she was going to be the Mother of God. Furthermore, the words spoken by the angel in God's behalf made her conscious of the fact that God had created her to be the Mother of the Messiah, of the long-awaited Savior. All her life, the part which was already past and that which was at that moment beginning, was bathed in a sudden torrent of light. Gabriel's marvelous and unexpected greeting already held a meaning for her; now she understood why she was full of grace; even more, why she was the only creature who was full of grace and why she had always been so sensitive to the slightest promptings of the Holy Spirit; she also understood the reason for her own particular gifts. All the minute occurrences that constitute the pattern of existence, and at the same time the whole of existence itself in its totality, acquired a new sharpness of outline, and under the spell of the angel's words everything took on a complete explanation more supernatural than metaphysical.

It was as if suddenly she had been placed in the center of the universe, beyond time and space. She knew God's plan from the Scriptures: the creation of the cosmos, the creation of life and the creation of man, the fall that destroyed forever the equilibrium of human nature, the promise of a Redeemer who would restore this equilibrium according to God's plan of salvation. The entire created universe was moved by superior forces in a progressive development of the divine plan. And with the rest of the universe, she too was ready to give glory to God with the praise and the purity of her heart, humble and concealed from the world, unknown, an anonymous and insignificant part of that universe. And one day she discovered that she was really a fundamental part of the universe, that she was going to be the Virgin who would conceive, the Virgin Mother prophesied for centuries. And her son was going to be God.

From this moment on, her position in creation was quite clear to her. She understood, as far as it was possible for a creature to understand, the purpose of history, the slow and inexorable realization of God's plan in the universe. Time past and time future assumed a new fullness of dimension and merged in this unique moment. The concealing veil was drawn back for her; God allowed her to participate in his secret; he revealed to her his fondest plan.

From now on her way would be very clear; it was determined by the Annunciation. The Annunciation, however, was merely a realization of the potentiality of Divine Maternity which she had always carried within her. The future was no longer hers exclusively; God himself was going to point out to her through a thousand unimportant circumstances what her attitude and her conduct should be at each moment and in each set of circumstances. She now possessed fully the general criterion that was to inspire all her actions, for every action will be in accordance with the nature of the agent. She was full of grace, and as soon as her *Fiat* was pronounced she became the Mother of the Savior. All that followed was merely the consequence of this *Fiat*, "Thy will be done."

Also, the meaning of all the past was revealed to her. Before she was born the prophets had already thought and written about her. When Adam and Eve sinned and were dispossessed of their gifts and expelled from Paradise, she, the Immaculate, was already present in the promise of God. She began to remember the history of the chosen people, and she understood it all.

How easy to understand everything now: from the height of her vision she was able to look back to the beginning of time's complicated weaving of events, very often confusion, and through all she could see the patient story of God's grace leading everything to the fullness of time without ever interfering with the liberty of men. How many things had had to happen: the patriarchs, the captivity in Egypt, Moses and the hard years in the desert, the conquest of the promised land, the Judges and the Kings, the Babylonian captivity, the fight of the Maccabees, until God's hour arrived. All concurred towards this decisive moment. All the past, since creation itself, had had some relation with her; all the future, everything that would happen up to the end of time, would also be related to her.

It was not a matter of chance that she came from the lineage of David and was betrothed to a man also from the house of David. Neither was it a matter of chance that she had been born in Judea, nor that her birth coincided with such happenings as the control of Judea by a foreign power or the coming Octavian peace: God had foreseen everything.

In this manner the Annunciation was, for the Virgin Mary, the key to all existence. God, by his own choice and without consulting her, decided her part in creation, and from the moment in which our Lady discovered her destiny, her life was one of complete illumination. This illumination extended through her entire life, giving her maturity and profundity and a singleness of purpose that enabled her to go through life doing her duty, ignoring the ups and downs of the world, so that no circumstances whatsoever would be able to touch her deep down or change her in any way. It is the same with all of us; whatever happens to us happens through the design of God.

There was never any monotony in her life, because every life becomes a great and passionate adventure when God takes possession of a soul and when a soul is willing to cooperate fully with God, accepting and fulfilling completely and without reserve whatever part the Creator has designated for it in the universe. When we make our will one with the will of God, when we let God take possession of us, life gains a purpose and is worth living; this unity of will between God and man eliminates all sense of routine, gives interest and meaning to the thousand small events of everyday existence: "That is why I have told you so often, and hammered away at it, that the Christian vocation consists in making heroic verse out of the prose of each day. Heaven and earth seem to merge, my children, on the horizon. But where they really meet is in your hearts, when you sanctify your everyday lives."[1]

---

[1] J. Escrivá de Balaguer, *Conversations*, no. 116.

If we wish to explain the Annunciation in a simple manner and in everyday language we could say that for the Virgin Mary the Annunciation was simply the discovery of her vocation. Obviously, when we ask ourselves about our Lady's vocation, the immediate answer is that her vocation was to be the Mother of the Savior. And she discovered this through the message of Gabriel.

Thus, suddenly, she comes before our eyes in history, like a flash of lightning, without any warning that she would so suddenly appear. The first news that we have about her is concerned with her vocation, and with this news our Lady enters into the narration of the Gospels. Of all the important things that can happen in our life, unquestionably the most important, that which illuminates and explains all the others, is our vocation. When we discover what our vocation is, we discover the true meaning of our life, the purpose of our existence. In order to develop a possible scheme for the imitation of our Lady in a precise and objective manner, the first thing we must examine is the problem of vocation.

Ordinarily, the word "vocation" is employed in a rather restricted sense to mean the call to consecrate oneself to God either in the priesthood or in the religious state, or in some other way. Thus we say that a person has no vocation when it is clearly obvious that marriage is the state of life indicated for such a person.

This limited concept of vocation gives the word a certain tone of compulsion, of renunciation, of something that is absolute, definite, and irrevocable and to a certain degree makes the word a bit frightening. It is not difficult, consequently, to observe among young people, young men and young women between seventeen and twenty-two or twenty-three, a certain attitude of reserve when faced with the possibility of a vocation; they are on their guard as if to defend themselves from some danger. Such an attitude is manifested (in those for whom the word means something, or at least in some of them) in a cautious avoidance of going beyond certain limits in their relations with God; he might demand too much; he might demand everything. In this way a certain insincerity, a deep-rooted and subtle falseness, very often unconscious, clouds their lives and frequently constitutes an obstacle to the fullness of their Christianity.

In a certain sense this jealous watchfulness over one's own independence, this instinctive fear of losing one's complete freedom, of having a vocation (in the sense already explained), is understandable when we consider the make-up of human nature. But if we amplify the meaning of the word "vocation," then the absurdity and irrationality of such an attitude becomes clear. Through a careful consideration of the verses from St. Luke's Gospel, quoted at the beginning of this chapter, it is possible to gain a more complete vision of the concept of vocation, a vision embracing all the various ways of life, a vision that shows us what the basic elements of a vocation are and consequently enables us to deduce certain practical and important lessons.

To begin with, it does not seem unreasonable that we should accept the Annunciation, the vocation of our Lady, as an archetype, and exemplary, of the phenomenon of vocation. The Virgin Mary is not only a creature, but the most perfect creature ever to have come from the hands of God. Her closeness to the Trinity—daughter of the Father, mother of the Son, and spouse of the Holy Spirit—places her on an exceptionally high plane very near the source of all grace, there where things show themselves with the greatest purity, with the least possible of those earthly influences which usually mask or shadow our visions of the supernatural. The phenomenon of vocation, then, appears to us in Mary in a pure state, diaphanous, without any impurities that might cause wrong impressions or confusion.

An analysis of the Annunciation opens up new perspectives for us, perspectives of great amplitude and enormous consequences. One can easily observe the existence of three distinct moments. There is, first of all, an announcement, a revelation of what God wants of her, of what her mission in life is—what we might call the revelation of her place in creation. Then there is a grasping on the part of the Virgin of the will of God, a conscious understanding of the place that had been designated for her in the world, a kind of penetration into the idea that God had of her mission in life. And lastly, Mary's acceptance of the Annunciation in all its implications, an acceptance that was complete, immediate, and absolute.

All vocations have these three phases: the announcement of the design of God, understanding of this divine will, and an answer, whether it be acceptance or refusal. These are the three elements which together constitute one fact or phenomenon, and it does not seem prudent, if we are to understand this fact properly, to stress only the third element, the answer. The answer follows something, follows a proposition or invitation that precedes it.

God's plan

The divine plan precedes the Annunciation. Before one receives any kind of communication, before one sees something, that something must already exist. The angel Gabriel, in exposing the divine plan to the Virgin Mary, the plan that God had prepared for her, is not talking persuasively but directly and sharply: "You *have* found favor with God . . . you *will* bear a son; and you *shall* call his name Jesus." He does not ask for her opinion; he announces facts that are soon to be fulfilled. Independently of her will and without Mary knowing anything about it, God has made his decision for her. It is the Trinity who has plotted out her future and who has gifted her abundantly in order that she may carry it out. The angel is simply a messenger, the means that God uses in order to make his decision known to her.

No one is an exception in this matter, and it is easy to understand even for people who seldom think in a supernatural manner.

God is infinitely wise; he foresees everything; he knows everything, and there is nothing that can escape his foresight. God knows everything that happens before it happens; everything that happens he either wishes or allows. Everything which is good, which is well ordered, he wishes it. He does not wish evil, sin, disorder, but he has made man intelligent and free—in his own image and likeness—and allows man to commit evil rather than deprive him of his liberty.

But God is infinitely intelligent, which supposes a purpose in everything which he does. And if anything which happens, no matter how small, is wished by God if it is good or allowed by him if it is evil, there is some reason and some purpose behind it. And since he is infinitely good, the end that God intends is always a good end, that is, his glory, to which the whole universe and each one of us is closely related.

The foresight of God, his intervention in animate and inanimate life, in the affairs of nature and the affairs of men, in all events and actions, is absolute, complete: "The very hairs of your head are all numbered." It is evident that if God cares for things of such trivial importance as the number of hairs on our heads, so much more will he care for things of major importance.

There are, therefore, two words that have only a very superficial meaning: chance and accident. They are admissible as words that refer to circumstances unknown to us at the moment, but it is impossible to give them real value inasmuch as we know that it is God who in the last analysis is arranging the events of the universe, even the smallest and those which appear most insignificant.

No one has been born by chance, and no one was consulted before being brought into the world. The essence and existence of each person is something of extraordinary value, something very important, so important that it bears a direct relationship with the blood of Christ, since when each person is born his soul has already been redeemed. Every birth is always the result of a very long, minute, and patient planning. A great number of circumstances, arising century after century, converge in the precise moment in which a new being, singular and unique, makes his entrance into the world.

And if no one exists by chance, there is no chance involved in his particular physical and psychological makeup. There is also a reason for the fact that everyone has his own individual temperament, qualities, a particular degree of intelligence, sensitivity, and even particular features. Underlying the circumstances which are the immediate explanation of a person's character at any given moment in his life—education, environment, friends, influences, reading—deep down that orderliness which there is, gives unity to the cosmos, linking the immense variety of different creatures. God neither maintains nor renews anything useless on the earth. Everything has a reason for being and existing and each creature has been appropriately gifted for the end which it is to fulfil in the universe.

This is what we can appreciate very clearly in the most perfect of all creatures. The reason for the Virgin Mary's whole being, for her whole existence, was her maternity. The qualities with which God had gifted her are explained and justified in relation to Christ, because she was to be his Mother. This is also the reason why God lifted for one moment the yoke that had weighed down mankind since Adam's sin, in order that not even original sin should touch her with its humiliating mark.

It certainly does not seem difficult to admit and understand God's plan regarding certain creatures. Instead of surprising us, on the contrary, it seems quite reasonable and logical that God should have gifted St. Paul so abundantly. Why not, since God had created him to be the Apostle of the Gentiles, one of the pillars of the Church? It would be inconceivable, on the other hand, that while the Creator is absorbed in preparing the path of some great saint, modeling his soul, giving him a mission, providing him on his path with sufficient grace to enable him to carry out his mission, he should neglect other souls that come into the world, failing to give them a certain place or part in creation, a certain road or mission. If that were true, then indeed one could justifiably speak of human beings as the victims of chance, without end or objects; God would not have foreseen anything concerning them. This possibility is absurd.

God does not consult anyone before calling him into being. It is he who thinks about us before we are born, who gives us our qualities, who gives us a certain degree of intelligence; it is he who chooses our parents and determines when and where we shall be born. It is he who plans our way, who gives us a task in the universe. It is God himself who has provided and arranged carefully a great number of small occurrences throughout our lives that will help to lead us, with our own cooperation, toward our designated goal.

It is the Christian outlook on life and on history that in the final analysis leads to an explanation, to an understanding of both. In the vocabulary of one who believes in Jesus Christ and in his words, the term "destiny" does not have that connotation of superior force which it acquires in the minds of those who need to believe in destiny because they do not believe in God or in his personal action (they must have some way in which they can explain the great and deep mysteries of human life). What the positivists or those who are indifferent in religious matters call "destiny" is the collection of precise and almost fatal events that happen to a person independently of his intervention. A Christian knows, however, that destiny is not a blind, unknown, and terrible force, but the action of God in the world.

The fact that destiny and God's design are the same thing becomes manifestly clear in the experiences of our lives when our intelligence analyzes the most profound sources of the events around us without passion or sophism or prejudice. This point is particularly well illustrated in the careful investigations of one of the most brilliant philosophical minds of contemporary Spain, whose analysis of his own experience was so thorough that it brought about a radical change in his entire life. I am referring to the investigations carried out by Manuel Garcia Morente, who was a professor of ethics and dean of the faculty of philosophy and liberal arts at the University of Madrid. Morente's strictly speculative analysis of himself dealt with the concatenation of certain events in his life. According to his own narration, a series of various events began to take place in his life at the beginning of the Spanish Civil War in 1936.

In his extensive work of such great human value he writes: "Since the beginning of the war I had not been in the least concerned with guiding the events of my own life; with the real texture of the facts of my own existence. My life, the facts of my life, had gone on apart from me without my intervention. In a certain sense I can say that I had seen the events of my life happen, I had been present at them, but had not caused them in any way. Who, then, or what, was the cause of my life which, being mine, was not mine? The unusual and curious thing about all this is that the happenings were facts of my life, that is to say, they were mine. On the other hand, however, they had not been caused, nor provoked nor even suspected by me: that is to say, they were not mine. There was an evident contradiction; on the one hand my life belongs to me since it constitutes the real historical content in time of my being; on the other hand, however, this life does not belong to me, it is not, strictly speaking, mine, since its content comes in each case produced and caused by something alien to my will. I could find only one solution to this paradox: something or someone distinct from myself shapes my life and gives it to me, ascribes it to my own individual being, attributes it to me. The fact that someone or something outside of me creates my life, explains sufficiently why my life, in a certain sense, is not mine. But the fact that this life made by someone else is given or attributed to me explains in a certain sense why I consider it mine. This was the only way to explain the contradiction or paradox between the fact that this life is not mine because someone else made it, although it is mine because I am the only one who lives it. . . . This life of mine, which I receive rather than make, is composed of events full of meaning." [2]

Certainly it is necessary that man should react to each of these events so full of meaning of which Garcia Morente speaks, but God's design precedes man's reaction; the divine plan is always ahead of us. And this previous phase of the Annunciation (the choice and creation of our Lady to be the Mother of Jesus Christ) is, if we consider it carefully, of great importance: it is not we who choose our vocation; it is the vocation that is given to us; all man does is receive it. Vocation is the plan of God for each creature, the mysterious choice that God makes for us to occupy a precise place in

[2] Iriarte: *Garcia Morente, Sacerdote*, pp. 70ff.

creation, always in relation to the divine plan. It makes no difference whether this part is big or small, glorious or humble, obscure or spectacular; what really matters is that it exists. Because this designation of the place we are to fill in the universe, this divine choice, is the key to all existence. "God's calling gives us a mission: it invites us to share in the unique task of the Church, to bear witness to Christ before our fellow men and so draw all things toward God. Our calling discloses to us the meaning of our existence. It means being convinced, through faith, of the reason for our life on earth. Our life, the present, past, and future, acquires a new dimension, a depth we did not perceive before. All happenings and events now fall within their true perspective: we understand where God is leading us, and we feel ourselves borne along by this task entrusted to us."[3]

An oversimplification—perhaps a too comfortable interpretation—of the idea of choice has made the problem of vocation purely personal, almost subjective.

Someone may think that a man who finds himself at a crossroads—one way leading to matrimony, the other to a complete consecration to God—if he is generous will decide to give himself to God and if he is selfish will decide on marriage. This is obviously an erroneous view because it makes the question of vocation merely a matter of generosity depending on each one's willingness to give himself: "All men take not this word, but they to whom it is given." A vocation, the design of God, in that case, if it were merely a matter of generosity, would never be decisive; it would lack strength; and the most important aspect of existence, the reason for each one's whole individuality and personality, the reason why each one of us was created, would become something purely accidental. Besides, such an attitude would deny the value of matrimony, which is a state and a sacrament, as a positive way that God wishes and that leads us to him; such an attitude would reduce marriage to a kind of condition for those who have no generosity, becoming a public mark of mediocrity.

---

[3] J. Escrivá de Balaguer, *Christ Is Passing By*, no. 45.

We are all born with a vocation, but not the same vocation. Of course, marriage exists as a natural and generic vocation for anyone who is physically normal; that is why God creates men and women and the attraction between the sexes. But to certain persons God assigns a task that demands the renunciation of this natural vocation for a higher vocation; God needs them free of preoccupations; so, far from imposing a heavy load on them (the complete renunciation of everything), what he does is to liberate them from certain ties, however noble and legitimate these may be.

It is of prime importance to be convinced on this point. Only a clear consciousness of a transcendent purpose can give unity and direction to a life lived in the inexorable passage of time through a thousand vicissitudes. We will be able to perceive that these vicissitudes have a real meaning only if we already know what purpose is behind them. This act of God upon us, before and above history, is the ultimate explanation of everything.

The message

God is the Lord, the Almighty. All creatures are his. But God is not a capricious being: order, measure, and proportion are maintained in all his works. The Virgin Mary was in his divine mind from all eternity, and from all eternity too, *ab aeterno*, God had settled the exact moment when the Word would become flesh in the pure womb of a woman. Both decisions were intimately related; the Annunciation was closely linked to the Incarnation and depended on it, and the Incarnation of the Son of God is the most extraordinary fact of creation and of history.

Here, too, God maintained a sense of proportion. He sent an exceptional messenger, the Archangel Gabriel, who was an attendant at the throne of God (Lk 1: 19); our Lady was also an exceptional creature—the only one free of original sin; and the message was likewise an exceptional one.

The very greeting is a part of what is going to come after it. It is important not to forget that Gabriel is only an emissary, a messenger, who himself has nothing to say to Mary.

His presence in the house at Nazareth is merely a consequence of his message-bringing. Gabriel is nothing more
than an instrument, an excellent one, of course, but at the
same time insignificant in the sense that he himself signifies
nothing, acquiring his importance merely as a functionary of
God who sent him. All his value at that moment is reduced
to the fact that he is a messenger of God. His greeting, consequently, is already a part of the message, the beginning of
what he has to say, and its purpose is to prepare Mary's mind
in some way—the most convenient and appropriate—for
the great revelation that is to come. Moreover, the greeting
in itself constitutes a revelation. Gabriel tells Mary that she
is full of grace, that the Lord is with her, and that she is
blessed among women. With this he starts to pull aside
the veil and give her knowledge of what God has entrusted
to her.

After the "Do not be afraid" has put her at ease, the fundamental part of the message comes: what God has decided
for her. What the angel says is certainly amazing but clear
and diaphanous. His first affirmation is noteworthy: "You
have found favor with God." Every vocation, every existence, is in itself a great grace that encloses within it many
others; it is a grace, a gift, that is given to us, that is bestowed
on us without our having deserved it, without being motivated by any merit of ours, and with no right to it on our
part. It is not necessary that the vocation, the call to fulfil the
plan of God, the assigned mission, be great or splendid. It is
enough that God has wanted to employ us in his service, that
he wants us to aid him, that he trusts in our cooperation.
The fact that he wants our cooperation is in itself so extraordinary and magnificent that an entire life spent in thanksgiving is not enough to repay him for such an honor. All of us
have already found grace in the eyes of God since we all have
received being and existence from him, and also a task, a part
to play in the divine plan, and we all have been bought at a
great price—we have cost the blood of Christ (1 Cor 6: 20).
Each minute of life is a grace, as is every apparently chance
encounter with other creatures.

Gabriel clearly revealed the plans of God to our Lady in a

language which she understood perfectly. The words used by the angel were unequivocal; they were the same words that the prophets had used in writing about the Messiah. The expressions were familiar to Mary. If we read the second book of Kings, for example, we find in reference to the Messiah: "And thy house shall be faithful, and thy kingdom for ever before thy face: and thy throne shall be firm for ever" (7:16). And Isaiah, talking about the miracle, says: "For to us a child is born, to us a son is given," and then "Of the increase of his government and of peace there will be no end. He shall sit upon the throne of David, and upon his kingdom: to establish it and strengthen it with judgment and with justice, from henceforth and for ever" (9:6). These and other messianic texts were well known to those who loved Scripture.

The first part of the message is really the most important, the most substantial. It is at this point that our Lady asks a question and what Gabriel next says is merely an answer, or, more appropriately, an illustration. It is probable that the first and second parts of the message are indivisible. The entire message had probably been prepared by God even before Gabriel visited the Virgin; God undoubtedly would not leave even the smallest part of such an important revelation to the free initiative of the angel, in spite of his superior angelic intelligence. If it seems that the angel's clarification is a perfect answer to Mary's question, we can perhaps attribute this to the Virgin's delicate intuition, her extraordinary sensitivity for things supernatural; when she interrupted the discourse of the angel with such an appropriate question, rather than interrupting what he was saying she facilitated its continuation. She was so prodigiously full of grace that she asked exactly what God had decided to reveal to her.

The message was complete in spite of its brevity; the message tells her what and how: what God has decided and expects from her, and how she is to bring it about. It is not, by any means, a detailed announcement; it is a question of communicating a fact of exceptional importance; in no sense is it a prediction of the future. There are no unnecessary details in the message, but in its brevity everything has been said, everything has been clarified; there are no loose ends, the angel even telling her about the Son who is to be born of her. She needed to know his name, his grandeur, his royalty, the eternity of his reign, because from then on he was going to be in her care. She could not cooperate blindly because she was to be an intelligent instrument.

The last part of the message that was unveiled to our Lady, the miracle which God had wrought in Zachary's wife, Elizabeth, was not exactly a sign or a test to make her believe in the message. Unlike Zachary, she who was full of grace did not require any confirmation in order to believe. On the contrary: this part of the message is also a revelation not of the mere fact of Elizabeth's conception, which Zachary could find out at any moment, but of the deep and secret bond that linked what had occurred in Elizabeth's life with what was going to occur in the life of our Lady. The angel had scarcely mentioned the relationship between both events when Mary's intelligence accepted and understood it perfectly. The events in which she was to play a direct part were thus deepened in her understanding, for she saw that God's prevision was also acting on other people in order to prepare the scene and make ready the world in which the announcement of the angel was to be fulfilled.

The final phrase, "For with God nothing will be impossible," is linked in the text with the allusion that the angel makes to the miraculous fecundity of sterile Elizabeth. This phrase can be interpreted both as a revelation of the benevolence shown by God to Elizabeth and as a genuine declaration of God's power in all things relating to the miraculous way in which he chose to give us his Son.

The angel's message to Mary was so extraordinary, so unheard-of, so far beyond the ordinary laws of nature and even beyond human comprehension, that this was more an ecstatic acknowledgement of God's power on the part of the angel than a test of Mary's faith. And with this final phrase, everything is completed. Nothing remains to be said, and the Virgin Mary now understands what God's will is for her.

God always has some purpose for his creatures. And God's message concerning them is something objective, something that exists in all men. The case of the Virgin was unique; it is not common for God to send such emissaries to men because vocations or destinies as important and decisive as hers are rare. It is true, however, that God at one moment or another of our existence speaks to everyone of us, not physically, not in a manner perceptible to our bodily senses, but in a thousand other ways.

If all creatures belong to God, it is possible for him to use them to talk to us. It is to God's decision concerning us that we owe our existence and our own individual being. God must let us know in some way our mission in life, what he wants and expects from us, the way that he has chosen for each of us to reach him. Logically there must be in all our lives a *revelation*, a moment in which God's will for us becomes recognizable.

But no one can expect the appearance of an angel, nor can we demand that God's will be made known to us accompanied by some objective evidence of its origin, or so simply that we need not make the slightest exertion to understand it. The will of God is shown to us through his creatures. It might be an event that makes an impression on us, it might be a conversation with a friend, a phrase, or the example of a certain person. Frequently it is not a sudden revelation but a small light which grows larger and gradually obliterates all the shadows of our doubts.

A special communication is not necessary—nor does it often take place—for the most common of all vocations there always exists *a priori*—we have already pointed out—the vocation of marriage. Marriage is, we can say, the most general of all calls, the natural vocation in which most men remain, although to adapt it to God's plan and to give it a true value it must be raised to the supernatural level. The fact that there is a natural inclination—a natural calling—toward this way of life makes any further summoning unnecessary. On the other hand, for those specific vocations that demand a renunciation, for the vocations that necessitate the sacrificing of noble and legitimate possibilities, God provides that his plan be revealed with sufficient clarity at some moment or other in life—at the opportune moment.

The various means God uses to reveal his will are most diverse, and it would be foolish and probably useless to try to enumerate what means God has used. In any case, it is not too much to say that every vocation implies a calling on the part of God to orient our lives in a certain direction, a call to serve him in a certain concrete way. But this calling, this message through which God lets us know his plan for us, our vocation, the place he wishes us to occupy in creation, must be objective. It is something that is outside of us, independent of us and our own wills, something apart from our subjective feelings and tastes, our whims and mere natural inclinations.

It is this note of objectivity, this independence of the individual, which is the most clearly and precisely seen in the Gospel. Our Lord passes by the table of the tax collectors and says to Matthew: "Follow me" (Mt 9:9). It is our Lord who chooses the first twelve, calling them unambiguously by their names. At the beginning, before the final selection, St. John tells us in the first chapters of his Gospel how the disciples act as real messengers, contacting others and bringing them to the Lord. "God draws us from the shadows of our ignorance, our groping through history, and, no matter what our occupation in the world, he calls us with a strong voice, as he once called Peter and Andrew: 'Follow me and I will make you fishers of men.'" [4]

In each specific case there is a proportion between God's message and the person in question: one is always adequate to the other. There is no fixed pattern, or uniformity, in the means God uses to reveal our vocation to us, as there is no uniformity in creation. God does not repeat himself, and each creature is unique. The message was brought to Mary by an archangel, as was appropriate to her dignity and the magnitude of the mystery that was to be communicated; and in that way also the Lord addresses each of us. The means of communication vary, because God takes into account more

[4] *Christ Is Passing By*, no. 45.

circumstances than we would ever consider, even in our most important matters. The individual temperament, the personal circumstances, a thousand other little factors make this decisive moment in the life of each man adopt many different forms, although it is essentially the same in all men. An apathetic person, for example, requires a very different treatment from someone of a willing nature. For some people it may be a tragedy or some great disaster that opens their eyes to perceive transcendent reality—and here the expression is literally exact, since they are made to see something which existed before, but which these people could not see. Others need exactly the opposite; the absence of all distractions of the senses that might disturb their peace of soul: they need a more intellectual, colder, and detached message. Generally speaking, of course, this is better; the vocation should never become confused with the affections or emotions—the more that the calling is stripped of elements alien to its essence, the better is the guarantee of its authenticity.

But the message, besides existing in every person, being adequate and objective, extrinsic of the man himself, is also intelligible. It seems quite clear, now, that the only extraordinary element in the Annunciation was the means used, (to wit, the Archangel, for the reasons already mentioned), to deliver the message. Our Lady learned what design God had for her in her own home, under normal circumstances, and on an ordinary day in her life. God, who is our Lord, does not need to be ostentatious, nor does he like ostentation. It would seem that the unique simplicity of God's being marks all his works with the same character of simplicity. God does not need to wait for some special psychological moment; on the contrary, it is precisely when a man is completely normal, in his ordinary life—which must not be confused with the "ordinary," superficial way in which many people live—that God usually communicates his message, when all a man's faculties are clear and when he is in an everyday state of mind. Only then can a man distinguish the extraordinary from the ordinary, what comes to him from outside himself, outside his normal state, and infringes to a certain extent on his normal existence.

It is always within the framework of our ordinary lives and in familiar circumstances that God gives us an indication of what he wishes us to do with our lives; the exceptions to this rule are rare. "Your human vocation is a part—and an important part—of your divine vocation." [5]

The message is always perfectly intelligible. This is perhaps the point which is most unequivocally settled by the Annunciation. The announcement that the Virgin Mary received was unambiguous. The archangel took expressions from Scripture which Mary knew referred to the Messiah, for she was well versed in revelation. There was no room for misunderstanding. The message is intelligible independently of our will to understand it. Later on we shall see the capacity that is required in the person in order to hear the voice of God, but the communication is always sufficiently clear to be perfectly understood. It is beneath the dignity of God to force someone into something that he does not completely understand.

The only ones who cannot hear the voice of God are those who are not open to communication, those who are so full of themselves that they have no room for anything else, and those who are so full of noise that they cannot hear other voices more delicate and more profound. But all this does not in any way affect the existence of the message.

The reception of the message

The second part of the Annunciation is our Lady's reception of Gabriel's message. The first words of the archangel's salutation surprise and disturb her. Anything extraordinary or unforeseen that affects us directly makes us momentarily withdraw into ourselves until our intelligence can collect itself and overcome our surprise. The Virgin was disturbed, she "considered in her mind what sort of greeting this might be."

When Mary first heard the words she took them into her mind and tried to fathom their meaning and purpose. This is

[5] *Christ Is Passing By*, no. 46.

the first moment of contact between the Virgin and God's message. She must have had a clear idea that something extraordinary was happening, because of the clarity of her intellectual faculties, uncontaminated by original sin, because of a special actual grace, or because of the mere physical presence of the archangel. If the same words had been uttered by any ordinary person in other circumstances, or with less solemnity, they would not have caused any disturbance or deserved any special attention. If the same words had been addressed to someone else, someone for whom they had not been intended, they would not have had any effect.

These words had such a strong effect because God had used an angel as messenger, because the person to whom they were addressed was the Virgin Mary, and also because they were so simply spoken, without anyone else being present, and without ostentation.

In a woman who was not "full of grace," or "blessed among women," the same salutation would perhaps have induced pride but not have caused any disturbance. Something within the Virgin must have enabled her to perceive immediately that this greeting was for her and that something unusual was going to happen in her life. This was a unique event, never before experienced, and in these rapid seconds, which passed so slowly, her whole being was moved by the expectation of finding out what was going to happen next. Already something hovered over her like dawn emerging from behind a cloud.

When God first contacts us, before any definite calling but simply with his opening salutation, which always precedes the decisive message, we are usually filled with an obscure and vague fear. There is something within human nature that resists everything total or final, all movement toward a point of no return. The prudence of the flesh of which St. Paul speaks (Rom 8:6), in opposition to the prudence of the spirit, is deeply rooted in our being, and it shows itself with strength and cunning during the most important moments in our lives, when we meet with problems that require decisive action. Normally this reluctance of the flesh is one of the strongest allies of the devil, whose hatred for God tries to make men rebel against the divine plan. This natural fear of finality, when the person comes in contact with God's persistent and increasingly clear call, can be observed in even the strongest personalities and always takes place at the exact moment at which the message is understood, even if it is in the preliminary stage. The reaction of Jonas to the call of God is noteworthy in this content; he flees from God physically; he wants to go very far away where he cannot hear God, where he can forget him and disregard him completely (Jon 1: 1–12). Isaiah shudders at the first moment of his vocation, when he is in contact with God for the first time (Is 6: 5); Jeremiah makes excuses when God calls him directly (Jer 1: 6); St. Paul was blinded—Jesus himself had to convert him by force (Acts 9: 3–4).

But the fact that Gabriel said to Mary, *Ne timeas,* "Do not be afraid," should be interpreted as the result of Mary's uneasiness rather than her fear or dread, because fear or dread of the divine was impossible for one so full of grace. Two different feelings converged in the soul of the Virgin: a natural feeling of uneasiness to an event that exceeded the purely human plane, and another feeling that was less instinctive but much more forceful. Because she had been conceived without original sin, our Lady's intelligence was exceptionally clear, and therefore she had a very precise understanding of the fact that she was a creature, created from nothing. Certainly the angel's message, brief but full of praise, produced in her a strange feeling that disturbed her. It was the feeling of one who had a precise appreciation of the enormous disproportion that existed between the slightness of her true value and the greatness of the praises addressed to her. In Mary's case, her deep realization of her condition as creature, as *ancilla Domini,* the handmaid of the Lord, the knowledge of the infinite gulf between herself and God, was the reason the angel's greeting disturbed her; she understood that God had bridged this gulf, going toward her or, better, attracting her to himself. The Lord was with her. She had always considered her own lowliness—this is the word used in the *Magnificat*—and Gabriel had greeted her as if she were full of grace. Mary, who considered herself the most insignificant of creatures, now heard herself called blessed among women by an archangel . . . and she was only a girl of fifteen.

She was not afraid of what was to come, of what God might demand from her. Rather than fear it was, to use St. Bernard's word, bashfulness. An innocent, pure, simple, re-fined girl of fifteen years, humble to the point of complete self-abnegation, suddenly sees herself praised in such a way. With the constant realization of her own nothingness and the grandeur of her Creator, suddenly she hears from the angel what seems to her exorbitant praise. This should not surprise us; Mary was not divine, but a human being, scarcely a woman; for every human being the contact with the supernatural is always overwhelming, especially as in the case of the Virgin, when there is nothing to lessen the shock. This bashfulness, this shyness and uneasiness is so beautiful; it reveals such great delicacy and such exquisite sensitivity.

Mary did not have much time to think about what Gabriel's greeting meant. As soon as the archangel noticed our Lady's perturbation, he put her mind at rest, and began to unfold to her the mystery. Our Lady immediately under-stood all that the angel was saying, although it is very prob-able that the same message would have been unintelligible to anyone else because certain spiritual qualities were neces-sary, which Mary alone possessed.

In the first place, she had what we may call a supernatural outlook. In effect, it was not a matter of understanding the simple grammatical sense of the words but, rather, the pre-cise meaning that God wanted them to convey. It was not enough to know the Scriptures without realizing that God had revealed in them a series of truths unattainable to man by his ordinary powers of reasoning. It was necessary to know of the promise of redemption by a Savior about whom the prophets had written, to know the implications of the expressions used by them, and to perceive what was hidden behind the expressions themselves. The prophecies, the Scriptures, are like a bridge between the supernatural and ourselves, and in order not just to take the words and ignore their ultimate significance, it is necessary to know of the existence of that supernatural reality. Perhaps a brief example from the Gospels will clarify what I am trying to say. When our Lord announced his Passion to his disciples for the second time, clearly saying "The Son of Man will be delivered into the hands of men, and they will kill him; and when he is killed, after three days he shall rise," the disciples, says St. Mark, "did not understand the saying" (Mk 9: 30–31). It is very probable that, like the disciples, any other person but Mary would not have understood so easily and so fully what the message meant; perhaps another person would not have understood it at all. Her delicate interior sensitivity, her deep sense of the supernatural, the continual habit of moving in intimate contact with everything that was divine (we must not forget her Immaculate Conception), her constant recognition of God's will, her delicate intuitive perception of the slightest movements of grace, all these things together enabled Mary to understand perfectly the words of the angel according as he spoke them.

Furthermore, only a heart as pure and as detached as our Lady's could be so completely receptive to the message. It is difficult to explain briefly what this disposition of soul is in itself. The word "sincerity" is not strong enough because of its connotation in ordinary speech. Purity of heart also misses the mark; perhaps we approach it a bit closer with detachment or disinterestedness. A person with imagination, someone who can dream and does dream, someone who has made plans for the future, who has hopes, who cherishes ambitions, a person who lets himself be carried away by tastes, affections, or impulses noble or elevated, but merely human, a person who is completely immersed in the world, would find it difficult to maintain such a pure outlook that he could recognize immediately the revelations of God about his future. It is essential to keep the heart detached from all the things except God. One must live according to that profound and meaningful principle of St. Francis de Sales: "Neither want nor refuse anything." There is also a revealing passage on this point in the Gospels: "If any man will do the will of him [God], he shall know of the doctrine, whether it be of God, or whether I speak of myself" (Jn

7:17). Only the man who wants to follow the will of God knows whether or not the message comes from God. Knowledge, then, in this matter is a result of disposition. Our Lady had always moved on a preeminently supernatural level. She alone could know so quickly and fully and easily the design of God contained in the message, for she alone from the time of her conception was at the complete disposal of God, without any other wish than to do his will.

The Virgin Mary understood what God wanted of her and how it was to be performed. The question that she asked and the quick and definite answer of Gabriel shows us that God had foreseen everything and that he already counted on her decision to consecrate herself to his service, completely and permanently. She saw clearly how the prophecy of Isaiah was to be fulfilled: "Behold, a Virgin shall conceive and bear a son: and his name shall be called Emmanuel" (Is 7:14).

Her virginity would be maintained undefiled, and still she would become a mother. She needed no sign. Her mind saw it all clearly. The angel still continued speaking his message, however, because there was yet more to be said; everything that she was listening to had a mysterious relation with the miraculous conception of John the Baptist. Elizabeth was part of the mystery because her fertility, so late in life from the human point of view, had been revealed to the Virgin in connection with the revelation of her own future.

The angel's message to the Virgin was a simple exposition of facts, but implicitly it contained a calling. At the same time that it revealed God's plans to her, it was also an invitation to her to occupy her place in the order of the universe, like a foundation stone in a magnificent building or a keystone in an arch. The manner in which the message was delivered: "you have found favor," "you will conceive," "you . . . will bear a son," "you shall call his name," "he . . . will be called": appears to be an express command which allows no alternative but to obey. But it is an order given with such delicacy, so respectful and appealing that it does not appear to be an order; it almost seems like a request. On one hand it is an order from our Lord to his *ancilla*, his handmaid, from the Creator to the creature, from the Omnipotent to the one who by herself is nothing and who depends completely on him; on the other hand one can perceive the tenderness of God the Father, full of love for the most obedient and selfless daughter that he could ever hope for; the tenderness of the Father who knows that Mary's only passion is to grasp God's smallest desires in order to carry them out, whose only ambition is to do anything that is the will of her Father. There was no need for any explicit question. Since Mary was born without original sin, our Lord found a marvelous sensitivity and delicacy among Mary's most intimate natural qualities, qualities that grew spontaneously within her and unmistakably marked everything she did. Delicacy is one of the beautiful virtues of those who are in love, and our Lady was in love with her Father, God. Nothing else was necessary.

Ordinarily, the first and last of the phases into which we have divided a vocation present little difficulty. No one sees any problem in the fact that the call to a vocation should be something objective, coming from outside the person being called, or in the fact that the call needs an answer. The delicate point here, and one that often becomes a real and worrying problem, is the taking cognizance of God's message, the "taking to heart" of our vocation. The subject and the object are both clear, but the difficulty lies in the connection between the two, in the realization and personal application of God's exterior calling on the part of the individual in question. It is true and indisputable that God has a plan for all his creatures. It is also true and indisputable that there must be a moment in the life of each man when God communicates his plan to him. It is further true that a Christian, indeed every human being, should accept fully the will of God as soon as he knows it. But how can one know whether this or that particular thing is, in fact, the will of God? This is the "defensive" question that a person frequently asks, either implicitly or explicitly, when he feels he is being overcome by someone stronger than himself: "How do I know that this is really a call from God and not a temptation or some transitory feeling or a momentary and fleeting impression? What guarantee have I that this or that particular person or event is the instrument that God is using in order to communicate his plan to me? What guarantee have I that such a person's message is an expression of God's will for me?"

This is a difficult phase, in which the objective and subjective come so close together that it often causes great interior suffering to distinguish where one ends and the other begins, to see which is which; a phase in which there is grave need for the light of God's word "more piercing than any two-edged sword and reaching into the division of the soul and the spirit, of the joints also and the marrow" (Heb 4:12). In this phase too, our Lady with her example and her attitude teaches us a profound lesson that can serve us as a guide.

A vocation to a complete renunciation supposes an equally complete change in a person's way of life. It means adapting ourselves completely to God's plan, leaving behind even very good and admirable aspirations because God has other plans for us, plans that are more elevated and better than all those things which have to be left behind; this renunciation, however, causes a natural resistance because our nature is so attached to those other things.

I have already spoken of the fear that young people have of the possibility of being called to serve God through a complete surrender of oneself—that is, the fear of vocation as it is commonly understood. This is to be expected. The fear of a vocation is logical, but it is illogical for us not to try to overcome this fear, to shut God's will out of our lives by becoming superficial and confused or by varying in our relations with him, instead of facing the problem and solving it with cheerful abandonment, trust, and submission to his will.

Very often God prepares in a slow and gradual way the souls of those whom he chooses to work solely for him. The angel's greeting to Mary was the preparation for the revelation of God's will concerning her, and the Virgin experienced uneasiness. This uneasy feeling of expectation or presentiment of something to come is also experienced by many souls for whom God has planned lives of sacrifice,

sometimes great sacrifice. From time to time one feels a
vague uneasiness without knowing why, since there is no
apparent reason for it; an uneasiness that does not come
from a sinful conscience because the conscience is clear, the
soul is in the state of grace and is in friendship with God. It
is as if the heart were tied with an invisible thread which
someone pulls at the most unexpected moments, at any
place and at any time. It is also like the feeling of emptiness,
of dissatisfaction, that a person sometimes feels, in spite of
the fact that he has everything he wants.

These feelings are not, in themselves, a sign that God is
going to ask everything; sometimes this interior restlessness
in people who live habitually in the state of grace is simply a
sign of secret pride, which obstructs complete peace; other
times these feelings may originate in something either in the
past or present which is not right in the eyes of God. At
most, if there are no natural causes such as sickness, fatigue,
or nervousness, these feelings should be carefully analyzed,
and we should seek the advice of a spiritual director; these
feelings may indeed be a preparation for God's calling us;
this might be how the Lord prepares us for the reception of
his message.

Behind all these things there is always a message concerning God's will in regard to us. Sometimes the message is that
we should rid ourselves of something that is troubling us
within and produces these feelings of uneasiness; at other
times it is that we should make straight whatever is crooked
in our lives and stops us from following the path of righ-
teousness; often the message is that we prepare our soul to
put itself at the disposal of God's will; it may be, too, that
these feelings are hints or presentiments that God is going
to talk to us so that we will not be over-surprised when we
learn that God has certain specific plans for our lives. This
obscure fear and uneasiness, this inexplicable inquietude,
these strange anxieties within us, this sensation of emptiness,
this dissatisfaction, this secret desire for something undefin-
able, this kind of satiation with the things that had until
now satisfied us, this profound disappointment with all the
things that we liked before, this slight and apparently absurd

uneasiness—all these things are very often the way God uses to turn our attention to his voice, while at the same time he slowly detaches us from the world around us.

This shock has very great intensity in exceptional cases. "The call to a great work on the part of divine providence truly means a great happiness and a great blessing, because it is a great manifestation of trust on the part of God; but for the man who is going to carry out this work it also means a heavy burden and a great amount of toil. This is the fate of the saints and the elect of God. God's friendship is at the same time God's burden."[6] The panic of Jonah at the prospect of having to go to Nineveh and to carry out God's mission is understandable.

There is no reason to be afraid. The angel put Mary's mind at rest: *Ne timeas*, "Do not be afraid." We should not be afraid of God or of the destiny that he himself has prepared for each one of us. The worst thing of all is the selfishness or the lack of alertness of those who do not see, either because they are unable or do not want to see. These people isolate themselves and cut themselves off from the voice of God, and, unable to find a purpose in life, direct it in their own way, creating their own purpose according to their own fancy; in this way a man loses all his chances of happiness and is left to rely entirely on his own strength in a whirlwind of exterior circumstances that oppress him on every side.

We must see. Whoever treats creatures (whether they be persons, things, events, instincts, impulses, or desires) as if they were opaque, beginning and ending in themselves, condemns himself to be the plaything of a thousand hands. Creatures for us must be of such transparency that we can see God behind them, a God who every moment expects something from us.

It is necessary to see: and in order to see we must have sight and light. It is necessary to have a certain interior sensitivity in order to see God's message in his creatures; a blind man cannot see. But even if one has excellent sight, one cannot see if one is surrounded by darkness. Light is neces-

[6] Joseph Holzner, *Paul of Tarsus*.

sary, a supernatural light which—as in the case of St. Paul—makes us blind to external things in order that we may have an interior vision of things, an intensity of such a degree as to allow one to see those hidden realities. For those who lack supernatural vision the whole language of creation is unintelligible. It remains merely so many words in which they find no meaning; they are like the disciples of our Lord who did not understand what he was talking about when he told them of his Passion. One frequently comes across this interior coarseness, this lack of sensitivity; and to remedy it is one of the most important tasks of confessors, educators, and spiritual directors. This lack of supernatural outlook, this way of living more or less apart from God, the excessive attention paid to the things that pass before us and vanish, with scarcely a glance for the supernatural realities that are to be discovered behind them, is the reason so many Christians destroy their lives on this earth and put their souls in eternal peril. There is light for everyone: God is light, and he is eternal. There is also a faculty that enables us to see, and ultimately those who do not see fail to see because they do not want to. In many cases, however, where there is no malice, we must ascribe the blindness to superficiality or preoccupation with the things of this world. It is very probable that if we Christians knew the Gospels—which unfortunately we rarely do—we would realize that, as in the case of the blind man of Jericho, our lives depend on the anxious and touching request: *Domine, ut videam!* "Lord, that I may see!" (Mk 10: 51). It is so sad not to see! One is so useless and unbearable when one cannot see!

The objective and the subjective are even more difficult to separate when it comes to the point of understanding the message intimately. The first and most necessary step is to penetrate into the very core of the message and understand completely what it means. What we need in order to apply the contents of the message to ourselves, to realize that what we see carries with it a delicate invitation from God, is the quality of detachment. We need detachment, too, when we accept the invitation, to fulfill what is expected of us and to follow the path God desires for us. The personal application in the case of the Blessed Virgin Mary was not a problem because she was full of grace and always moved with complete spontaneity toward anything which her extreme interior sensitivity showed her to be the will of God. We, however, have been born in sin, and the triple concupiscence grips us—at times with great force—and becomes a heavy burden that hinders our agility in moving toward God. It would seem, therefore, that those who are spiritually closest to God are those who with least effort and most consistency face the problem of vocation squarely and accept it as soon as they see what it is.

Here, too, is where human prudence enters in most subtly. The natural resistance to all that is final and irrevocable offers thousands of apparently logical and weighty reasons, excuses, and arguments. Sincerity with oneself is fundamental here, so much so that without sincerity we can hardly hope to acquire interior peace; for here we are closer than at any other time to the danger of deceiving our own consciences. There are minor attachments, petty interests, and subtle excuses that prevent our complete sincerity in putting the problem before us exactly as it is. "How difficult it is for a man to extract the practical consequences of his intellectual convictions when they demand a sacrifice! How long is the road from the head to the heart!" (Holzner).

It is the heart which now intervenes, and the heart does not think: it only desires. The most difficult and painful moment comes when our inner being is torn apart by the tension of two strong and opposing internal forces: the intelligence, which sees, and the heart, which does not want to see and resists. Here human nature damaged by original sin appears with all its faults; it weighs us down, tying us to the things of sense and awakening in us a thousand screams that drown out the voice of God calling us. Deep within us, nevertheless, we, as it were, sense and feel the reality of the call; at the same time we feel an instinctive fear of facing the problem as it comes, for then we would also have to accept all its implications and to solve the problem completely. Thus we often try to resolve this internal unrest and tension by examining the signs and symptoms of vocation and the implications of the total renunciation it demands; instinctively we look for something to satisfy our intelligence, avoiding what it is difficult for nature to accept. It is then that we give artificial importance to things that have no importance in themselves and that we have heretofore considered unimportant; we become confused and refuse to take into consideration the fact that vocation does not depend on physical makeup or nervous system or the state of our digestion. Our physical makeup, may, however, indicate that we do not have a certain kind of vocation.

One seeks a sign, some human evidence, forgetting that a vocation is not simply a natural fact but, rather, a supernatural reality. This does not mean, however, that the intelligence, the reason, have not their part to play.

The Church, with the wisdom and experience of age, has set down certain conditions or signs without which there can be no authentic vocation: it is necessary to have rectitude of intention, to be suitable, to be accepted. This last condition is the most delicate, because it leaves the ultimate interpretation of the message to human beings with all their load of imperfections and failings. Hence that margin of time which is always allowed as a test before final acceptance, for these human beings need not only an upright conscience but also a deep knowledge of the individual in each case, what in medical terms is called the "clinical history," and an understanding of all facts relevant to a proper judgment of the case. Hence also the responsibility of confessors and spiritual directors, whose task it is to give good advice, because it can happen that their own feelings interfere with and even interrupt the action of the Holy Spirit. It is well to remember the words of St. Thérèse of the Child Jesus in her autobiography: "It is absolutely necessary to forget your own tastes and personal opinions, and to guide souls, not according to your own way of life, but according to the way of life pointed out by Jesus."[7] Momentary negligence, a human outlook, a rash decision—these things may change a path and ruin a vocation.

[7] *Story of a Soul*, chap. 10, no. 11.

Furthermore, the reception of God's message is often not received all at one moment, because the message itself is often revealed gradually. Perhaps the most characteristic case is that of St. Paul. When he surrendered himself to God and asked: "What wilt thou have me to do?" the Lord merely said that he should go to a certain place, where he would receive instructions (Acts 9:6). From then on God gradually let Paul know what he expected of him, at times through his own agency, at other times through the agency of the Church, until at last his mission as apostle of the Gentiles was revealed to him. It is only by being faithful to the little whisperings of God, it is only by following the impulses of grace with great docility, that we are finally led to the fullness of our vocation and the discovery of the object of our existence. Some arrive at this discovery slowly and smoothly, without any anguish; others, perhaps because they are too attached to creatures and to their own judgment, have to pass through fearful interior trials, and they reach their goals only after they have experienced great internal darkness and tempests that strip them of the impediments that were tying them to earthly things and remove the clouds that dim their sight.

The answer

It is very difficult to penetrate the most intimate sentiments of the Blessed Virgin during those moments, but it would seem that in an incredibly short time she passed from a state of uneasiness to one of absolute serenity. There was no resistance in her nature to the word of God. Calmed after the *ne timeas*, "Do not be afraid," with full understanding of everything contained in the words of Gabriel, as soon as he had ended his revelation, her answer was clear and distinct. It was a short, concrete and quick answer: "*Ecce ancilla Domini. Fiat mihi secundum verbum tuum*. Behold, I am the handmaid of the Lord; be it to me according to your word." There was no hesitation, not a moment's doubt. Neither did she ask for time to think it over before making up her mind.

She did not ask for time, nor did she need it. Doubt or

hesitation supposes indecision on the part of the will, but there was no room in Mary, who was full of grace, for indecision concerning God's will. "What had she to reflect about? Certainly not about the authenticity or reality of the message, because it contained nothing equivocal nor obscure to her. Neither had she to reflect about the consequences if she accepted the message, nor the consequences if she refused: to consider the consequences of acceptance would have been to go beyond what God intended her to see; consideration of what would follow from her refusal would have implied calculation. It is absurd, however, to think that the Virgin could be a calculating type of person, in the sense of carefully weighing the risks that giving herself to God would imply and judging whether the compensation would be sufficient. It is absurd also to think that the Virgin would hesitate to abandon herself to God's will. If ever there was anyone who had a vital link with the divine will, even in its slightest manifestations, it was the Virgin, conceived without sin.

The fact that the affirmative answer was so quickly given does not imply that it was given lightly. Those who are thoughtful by nature do not lightly give answers to serious questions. If we are to understand Mary's answer in all its depth, we must again consider it in the light of her uniqueness, and especially of the fact that she was born without sin. For an explanation of the most characteristic reactions of our Lady we must look to the fact that her being was completely untouched by sin, original sin and all other sin. It is difficult for us to understand with what degree of spontaneity the two highest faculties that man possesses, intelligence and will, united themselves in our Lady with their proper objects, Truth and Good. But only by considering the Virgin's will and intelligence united to Good and Truth in the very highest degree can we explain her quick understanding of the message and her firm adhesion to God's invitation.

The Virgin accepted not only the fact of her motherhood, but also the natural and supernatural changes that would be wrought in her and all the consequences that would flow from being the Mother of the Savior. She was acquainted with the mysterious words of Isaiah in reference to the Redeemer as a man of sorrows, covered with insults and bruises, torn apart by our iniquities. The idea of a bloody redemption, of a messianic kingdom very different from that cherished by her Jewish contemporaries, was not strange to her; her deep understanding of the Scriptures, indeed, must have been one of the things that isolated her and set her apart from the mentality of her own people. In spite of what she knew, nevertheless she accepted her vocation completely. And what is more, it was precisely her deep knowledge of the messianic prophecies which made her answer absolutely complete, embracing an understanding of all the vicissitudes, joys, and sorrows that would come from her being joined irrevocably with the Messiah.

There is, moreover, a certain tone of resolution in the pronouncing of the word *fiat*, "be it done unto me"; the Virgin's answer is definite and final; its force impresses us. It is more than a simple "yes." Once the request was answered, there could be no subsequent changes of heart; it demanded a complete submission of the will; an abandonment of herself, not to do some specific thing, but to do all the things that God had planned for her in exactly the way that he intended that they should be done; she was asked to renounce completely the right to plan her own life. All this concerned her in a direct and personal way, not as one who would bring about these things, but as the one in whom these things would be brought about. The *fiat* is much more than merely allowing something to be done; it is a determined and resolute adherence to the plan of God; it is a positive act of the will by which she willed the fulfilment of all that God had decided; not without thinking of herself, but accepting once and for all everything that the future held for her no matter what it should be.

The fact that the acceptance was preceded by the *ecce ancilla Domini*, "behold the handmaid of the Lord," gave an even more definite character to the answer. The clear realization of her relationship with God, of her position as a servant of our Lord—a handmaid—even more clearly illuminates the meaning of the *fiat*. She was there in order to serve, because she was a handmaid; servants do not ask their masters questions and demand certain conditions from them; they simply accept their job and do it. Everything that the Lord wants done must be done; in the case of the Virgin, however, it was more than this: she was linked to God so closely that she identified herself with his plans and she loved them with all the light of her intelligence and all the firmness of her will.

She was the handmaid of the Lord, but free, with a sovereign freedom, surpassed only by the freedom of her Son, who was God. It may seem to some that circumstances weighed so heavily on our Lady that in some way her will was undermined and she was forced to her decision. It can appear this way, however, only in the eyes of those who limit their idea of freedom to a purely natural sphere, a sphere in which an erroneous idea of freedom is often held, in which servitude is often mistaken for freedom. It may seem to these people that the extraordinary character of the Annunciation and the physical presence of the archangel must have exerted a certain supernatural coercion of her will and compelled her to accept instantaneously the angel's proposition.

Such a view, however, cannot stand up under analysis, especially when the concept of "freedom" is exactly understood. Freedom is not the same as independence. The Immaculate Conception of our Lady and the absence of all sin in her soul united her supernaturally to God from the moment of her creation, linked her to the Creator and bound her closely and firmly to the Being who was absolutely free. This is the root of Mary's sovereign decision, because "we are free in the exact proportion to our capacity for loving the beings and the things on which we are dependent. The extent of our freedom is identical with the extent of our capacity for communion . . . the saint, who can love everything, feels free everywhere and in all circumstances; those who are incapable of affection and sympathy, who are incapable of uniting with other beings, find slavery everywhere. Saint-Exupéry used to say that a man's worth can be measured by the number and kind of his attachments; to be free is to adhere interiorly and spontaneously to the unity which contains and surpasses us; it is to maintain relations with that unity similar to the relationship which a member maintains with an organism of which it is a part. Freedom means nothing in itself; its value is the value of man and the value of man is measured by the intensity of his being and the depth of his love." [8]

Because the Virgin Mary was closer to God than any other creature she participated more directly and with greater intensity than anyone else in the supernatural or divine life. Her possibilities of communion, of union, with God were consequently immense, and because she was so close to God and so dependent on him she was able to exist and act independently of all creatures. This spontaneous inner attachment to the will of God, this submissive and loving acceptance of her place in the unity that contained and at the same time surpassed her, was the most conclusive expression of her perfect freedom. If freedom, in the last analysis, is measured by the intensity of being and the depth of love, then this *ecce ancilla Domini* is the most complete manifestation of freedom, because the ultimate essence of each man in which all freedom is rooted is the fact that he is a creature of God.

Mary's answer, so brief and direct, without hesitation or doubt, without a moment's reflection, is incomprehensible to our mentality; it may even seem daring and presumptuous. To commit oneself so suddenly to an enterprise of such magnitude without assessing one's own potentialities and the complications that might develop is something that seems to us rash and irresponsible, indeed, madness. One is immediately reminded of the Gospel passage in which our Lord asks us to be prudent, when he speaks of the folly of the landlord who, before beginning to build a house, fails to consider whether or not he will be able to finish it; or when he speaks of the king who does not take account of the strength of his forces or compare his strength to that of the enemy before going into battles (Lk 14:28ff.).

---

[8] Gustave Thibon, *What God Has Joined Together*.

One may think that such a sudden, indeed immediate, decision in such an important and far-reaching matter is, at least, a lack of prudence, a sign of frivolity. On the other hand, no one would think of accusing the Virgin Mary of sinning through imprudence, through thoughtlessness or rashness, in immediately accepting God's proposal which is implicit in the angel's message. On the contrary, the answer she gives and the rapidity with which she gives it seem logical; the answer seems clear and proper, and we applaud it for its perfect reasonableness.

The various considerations of this single event, these seeming contradictions, have an explanation, however, since in each individual case we have to move on a different level. This full and complete acceptance, which at the same time was so prompt, may seem frivolous if the problem to be decided concerns any of us. In reference to the Virgin, however, it seems to us completely reasonable and makes perfect sense. On a purely abstract and theoretical level, as a simple speculative exercise, there is nothing to prevent us from arriving at conclusions of radical and extreme nature—that is, on the purely theoretical plane without any reference to real life. The difficulties arise, however, when we try to apply our conclusions to our own personal case and not to any mere fiction. Here we are vigorously confronted with the real nature of man, with all its defects and weaknesses. Because the fact of vocation, as we have by now come to understand it, is not substantially different in the Virgin Mary, a creature, and in us, also creatures, there is no essential difference.

It is the marks of original sin, left to human nature as a sinister legacy, which impede the free and spontaneous response of the soul to the divine invitation. Sensuality and greed, pride in all its forms, and the natural desire to achieve a happiness imagined by our own ego—all these are so many ties that block the supernatural impulses of obedience to God. But the rebellion is not usually open opposition, at least in many cases; instead it comes hidden under various disguises, one of the most insidious being that which conceals the problem from us, persuading us not to make a decision, which comes just before we recognize the problem, as already mentioned.

Once we have had a clear glimpse of God's will, the decision, as we have learned from our Lady, ought to be immediate, complete, definite, and completely free. A partial, irresolute, provisional, or halfhearted answer is futile as well as false, for it resolves nothing but only increases the period of uneasiness all men experience when they try to fathom absolutely the complexities of their own inner being.

Against an immediate answer, there is the temptation to delay. Here again we turn to some lines from Joseph Holzner, lines which, although they were written about St. Paul, have a universal value because of their theological intensity. "If one comes in contact with Christ and the supernatural world and waits for a more opportune moment, the longer one waits the more unlikely it is that that moment will ever come. Every delay hardens the heart."

Basically, every delay, "every putting off" of a decision which God demands of us, has its roots in a form of cowardice and springs fundamentally from fear of change; one is afraid of disrupting the tranquillity of one's own little world. Facing the unattractive prospect of suffering—for every vocation to give up something appears as a call to suffering— nature unconsciously prompts the person to delay the final acceptance in order to gain time to ease the tension or cure it altogether; such delay, however, is dangerous precisely because it represents a divergence between nature and grace. This time gained by hesitation allows the dark destructive forces of sin to gain a foothold within us; these destructive forces may, in the end, bring about the victory of nature over grace and suffocate at its birth the *fiat* that would have decided the future destiny of the person in the sense that God had planned it.

It is on this point that we can best appreciate the advisability of a serene and objective decision. As the decision of the Virgin Mary was at once rapid and serene, likewise anyone else's decision when he is called by God should neither be greatly delayed nor given lightly or flippantly. Here we can see the importance of a solid interior life based on a great sincerity with God and with oneself, enabling one to have a clear vision of our condition as creatures of God and at the same time a realization of God's plan, from which each creature derives its purpose. It is one thing to work with enthusiasm, which, of course, is excellent, when we believe in what we are doing, but it is a very different thing to work because we feel enthusiastic about something. Enthusiasm is a feeling and as such it is changeable, and because of this, everything that is built on as unstable a foundation as mere enthusiasm is destined to crumble and fall when the enthusiasm disappears. The time to wait is before, and until, we perceive the will of God; but once we have seen what his will is, then our immediate answer should be *serviam*, "I will serve," *fiat*. The best moment to decide is just when we can clearly see what our road should be, when God inflames the heart for the reception of the message; if we let this moment pass by we may be distracted by the world around us, made a prey of our own egotism and the temptations of our fallen nature; all these things blocking the entrance in our souls through which grace had for one moment entered so abundantly. Delay is the door which allows an easy entrance to many other temptations into the center of the soul, and it is particularly dangerous when the delay is conscious, when it is a voluntary postponement. For it is part of God's plan that we should have to struggle to serve him, and so, as a result of the damage done to our nature by sin, the natural resistance to such demands is quite human. This, in effect, explains why such a struggle should take place, something that would remain inexplicable without this intimate contradiction in each man, or, in the words of St. Paul, two men, the old and the new, who strive with each other for their mutual annihilation.

There is a temptation which urges us not to give ourselves completely, and it is what we might call the temptation of "inconvenience." Fundamentally, it consists in taking into consideration a multitude of purely human circumstances that in some way could be a kind of impediment and that could hinder us from giving ourselves completely to God.

They are reasons of an exterior type, which come to us from outside, but—and here lies the power of this temptation—which find a certain accomplice in each of us, because in these circumstances there is a strong impulse in nature to use as many weapons as possible to justify an attitude that is basically wrong. Generally, for those who have a certain interior depth, most of these external, trivial circumstances mean little. The most delicate and natural of all these circumstances, one which is quite within the order established by God and which carries enormous weight, is that of the family.

The opposition or the misunderstanding of relatives, and especially of parents, is, without doubt, the circumstance that causes the most bitter pain in a person who is going through this spiritual conflict, because the link with one's parents often appears to the person involved as a duty in conscience, especially if the parents have made plans for their children and have hopes and ambitions about their future or, even worse, if they need them in some way. Only by continuing to consider this problem, even in such trying moments, from the point of view of God, and relying on his grace, can such difficulties be overcome. For God knows and has always known, much better than ourselves, these family circumstances, or even opposition, which seem to impede our definite answer, and seeing them he, nevertheless, calls us. It is impossible that God should err or fail to take everything into consideration; all the inconveniences fall within his plan: he counts on them, and they are parts that have a positive function. It is important to realize this clearly, because there is a most subtle danger of fitting or adapting the call of God to the circumstances the world creates around us. One tries almost surreptitiously to replace God's will by another that is not exactly his; one takes his will and smooths off the rough edges, makes certain substitutions, depriving it of that very thing which often gives it the stamp of divinity—the Cross—and one ends up by making the divine will fit the limitations prescribed by one's own ego. The self-surrender then is not complete, for one does not surrender everything. God has more claim than anyone else on us and on everything that he has given us, and if he demands everything we should give him everything, even family, parents, reputation, honor, and life itself. One cannot haggle or bicker about giving up this thing or that, no matter how dear it may be: "Anyone who understands the kingdom Christ proposes, realizes that it is worth staking everything to obtain it. It is the pearl the merchant gets by selling all his property; it is the treasure found in the field."[9]

Now it would be well for us to make a few observations concerning the element of "irrevocability," the finality which every answer to God's call should have. Hernán Cortés, in order to assure the conquest of America, and so that his men might not be tempted to desert, burnt his ships ... but he kept the tools with which he could build new ones. In this case, merely burning the ships was not conclusive.

Any surrender of oneself to God that does not completely lay aside, from the moment of accepting the divine will, all thought and hope of retracing one's steps is false down to its very roots. To give oneself to God and at the same time to cherish plans, dreams, or projects, however vaguely or theoretically or dimly, which are outside the way one has chosen, is not to give oneself to God at all. It is too much like looking back when one has put one's hand to the plough;[29] it is like looking out of the corner of our eye at a future we might have chosen if God had not come to us with his all-encompassing demands. There is, it is true, a period in which the person can approach the vocation, in the vocabulary of the religious orders, in a provisional manner. This period could properly be called a period of formation, or preparation, because it is not so much a time for testing the reality or sincerity of the vocation as for preparing for God the instrument he needs, according to the way he himself indicates by giving a vocation to this or that specific way of life.

In any case, if a person's attitude is sincere, all paths except the one he accepts when he gives his *fiat* are conclusively ruled out. Later we will see to what extent the theological

<hr />

[9] *Christ Is Passing By*, no. 180.

virtue of faith plays a fundamental part in all the steps of the vocation, and in defeating all these types of temptations.

Finally, the decision should be free. Here too lurks another characteristic temptation: compulsion; not physical, of course, but moral. The temptation is not, as it may seem, that there may be compulsion in accepting the vocation and giving oneself to God, but the feeling after the acceptance that one was not free at the time of accepting; it is this specter of doubt that disturbs the soul and provokes a state of confusion and restlessness that robs the person of peace. It is rare to find a case in which moral compulsion weighs so heavily on a soul as to force someone to a decision contrary to the one he knows is right. The makeup of this temptation is very different, because it ordinarily appears as a confusion caused by the forceful influence of some other person whose personal power creates an atmosphere that tends to overwhelm and subjugate. Furthermore, since the existence of various influences around a person is an actual fact, the phantom of moral compulsion takes on a certain air of reality, which makes one seriously consider factors that should be disregarded by any sane and well-balanced person.

From the moment that we admit—as we must admit, since it is a fact—that man is a social being and consequently open to all kinds of influences, we see that he can be influenced just as easily in one direction as in another. Every life is subject to opposing forces and evolves in a state of tension which can ultimately be traced back to the opposition between nature and grace. The word "freedom" introduces many problems of all kinds; leaving aside the theological problem, the deepest of all, which deals with the coordination of divine omnipotence and human liberty, we can see that even a consideration of the human tendency toward imitation and mimicry is enough to provoke a thousand questions. To go even further: one can never find liberty in a chemically pure state, free of every kind of influence, because in an intelligent being the will tends toward that which the intelligence presents to it as good, and freedom—naturally—has a tendency to decide in the same way as intelligence and will. Every thought has a tendency to influence freedom, since freedom is a characteristic of intelligent beings.

One comes, then, to the conclusion that, since freedom is not independence, the same considerations that apply to moral compulsion in case of a decision to give oneself to God apply also when a person decides to give himself, for example, to a woman in marriage, that is to say, in another kind of vocation. The difference lies in the fact that all the forces of instinct tie us to the world, and the absolute giving of oneself to God has to overcome this strong attraction of nature. Otherwise, only those who lack personality, who are humanly weak in will and intelligence, will allow themselves to be compelled by others in these matters, and certainly this type of person does not seem to have the minimum of conditions necessary for a superior vocation. "The Lord does not destroy man's freedom; it is precisely he who has made us free. That is why he does not want to wring obedience from us. He wants our decisions to come from the depths of our heart." [10]

The meaning of life

Everything that has thus far been said, even the reflections on the Annunciation suggested by the verses of St. Luke, is closely related to one of the most important of all the problems that affect human beings, Christian and non-Christian. It would not, therefore, be out of place to deal more fully with some of the questions already raised and discuss them from different angles.

Reference must be made here to St. Josemaría Escrivá de Balaguer, the founder of Opus Dei, whose teaching has opened up so many prospects to the spirituality of the layman and has greatly influenced the orientation and content of this book as well as the author's own life. To begin with, two brief considerations from the excellent little book *The Way* situate the problem of vocation—taken in its widest sense—on a high and transcendental level that cannot be

[10] *Christ Is Passing By*, no. 100.

ignored. After explaining the condition laid down in the Gospel for entrance into the Kingdom of Heaven—fulfilling the will of the Father—he adds: "Many great things depend—don't forget it—on whether you and I live our lives as God wants. We are stones—blocks of stone—that can move, can feel, that have completely free wills. God himself is the stonecutter who chips off the edges, shaping and modifying us as he desires, with blows of the hammer and chisel. Let us not try to draw aside, let us not try to evade his will, for in any case we won't be able to avoid the blows. We shall suffer all the more, and uselessly. Instead of polished stone suitable for building, we will be a shapeless heap of gravel that people will trample on contemptuously." [11]

We are in the world for some purpose; everything that exists has some function. Creation is not a mere aggregation, a juxtaposition of beings, but a magnificent structure which has a unity, a reason, and a purpose for existence, a whole arranged on various different levels, from the inert stones to the angels who serve before the throne of God (Josef Pieper). Nothing that exists is useless. There is more truth in the old saying "While there's life there's hope" than we ordinarily attribute to it. The reason is, precisely, that God does not maintain anything useless on earth, and while man exists in time he can be certain that there is something for him to do that justifies his existence, a duty that binds him to God.

The fact that creation is not a mere conglomeration of beings but a well-ordered and harmonious unity explains the different vocations. Every soul has its own path, but it is also like a link of a chain, and it is connected with other beings. Therefore, to leave the will of God unfulfilled carries with it a great responsibility, because vitally important things may hinge on the fulfilment by each of us of God's plan. That also explains why men receive different amounts of grace, for it is God himself who, like a stonecutter with blocks of stone, works on man, with his cooperation, to form him in perfect proportions. Each man's graces are already provided before

---

[11] *The Way*, nos. 755–56.

his birth and distributed all along his way. These are the "blows" of God that lead man through this life to eternal life if he knows how to adapt them and fit them into God's plan. If man resists these "blows," he rejects grace and, since the blows are bound to come in any case, instead of forming they only deform him. It is impossible to conceive a more disjointed and unsteady life. The full cooperation of our Lady from her childhood with the slightest suggestion of the Holy Spirit enabled her to increase her original grace to such an extent that when God called her she was so full of strength and supernatural feeling that she gave herself up immediately to the will of her Creator; and something of vital importance did, in fact, depend on her readiness and her acceptance.

The discovery of one's personal vocation is the most important point in anyone's existence. It changes everything without changing anything, in the same way that a landscape, without changing, is different before and after the sun goes down, beneath the light of the moon or wrapped in the darkness of night. Every discovery gives a new beauty to things, and a new light creates new shadows; one discovery is the prelude to other discoveries of new lights and more beauty. This is what breaks the monotony of life; no one has lived as joyfully as the saints; no one has enjoyed life more; for the saints, life becomes really exciting, like a beautiful poem or a superb symphony. "All happenings and events now fall within their true perspective: we understand where God is leading us, and we feel ourselves borne along by this task entrusted to us." [12]

The two points from *The Way* previously mentioned show the seriousness of the problem and consequently the immense responsibility that hinges upon its solution. The natural and instinctive fear of a vocation that demands total surrender is understandable. But we should not allow this fear to cause any separation, however slight or however "precautionary," between God and us. It is a dangerous and false attitude for us to avoid getting too close to God for fear

[12] *Christ Is Passing By*, no. 45.

of finding that he wants to take possession of us completely and make us give up the plans, hopes, tastes, and projects that we were cherishing without consulting his will. This attitude is false because it does not regard truth and reality as they are. If God has chosen us from among innumerable creatures to fulfil a specific part in creation, this is a fact we cannot change; the only attitude worthy of a man in such a case is to accept things as they are, because they do not depend on us, nor will they change simply because we pretend to ignore them.

As well as being false it is dangerous. This attitude of closing one's eyes and taking refuge in a pleasant and comfortable shade in order not to see too clearly calls to mind the terrible phrase of Isaiah that St. John mentions in reference to the attitude of the Pharisees: "He has blinded their eyes and hardened their heart, lest they should see with their eyes and perceive with their heart, and turn for me to heal them" (Jn 12:40). If one chooses to close one's eyes, they may become closed forever: false blindness may become real.

Again, this attitude may lead us ultimately to be, in fact, blind to the path God has marked out for us, so that we go along another of our own choosing, according to our own wish and taste. Then we have mistaken the way, and the words of St. Augustine are precisely applicable: *Bene curris, sed extra viam!* "You run well, but off the road!" There is, then, a reversal of values, in which we put our own will above the will of God in a matter which, more than any other, determines the pattern of our entire life. A man is then a complete misfit. It is something similar to what happens to a body when a bone is out of place: it is dislocated, and it hurts. Life also hurts and becomes burdensome when one is out of place and destroys the harmony of the divine plan, living one's life outside God's design and purpose. Then only the humble acknowledgement of our own guilt can again give us peace. Our guilt is that of *non serviam*, "I will not serve," by which we prefer our own will to God's and refuse to submit to his. The humble acknowledgement of our guilt leads us to the immediate consideration of how to make reparation to God, and from this comes a willing acceptance of the pain the dislocation produces; and the pain thus accepted becomes a cross, and the cross that is loved and embraced is the road to salvation. It is not in vain that God is a Father, with bowels of mercy (*Deus noster, Deus salvos faciendi!* "Our God is the God of salvation," Ps 68: 20), for whom "nothing will be impossible" (Lk 1: 37). There is never any reason, nor is it reasonable, to be shy with God: here we are speaking, of course, from the supernatural point of view, the view of Christians. Vocation is not something dreadful against which we have to defend ourselves; on the contrary, it is the very *raison d'être* of our whole being and existence; it is the palpable proof of the love that God the Father feels for us. We are not useless beings abandoned to the whims of fate, without direction or guide, like the hopeless characters in the novels of Steinbeck, Faulkner, and many others. St. John teaches that God is love, and we are the fruit of that love. God has planned a future for us, and he has gifted us generously and fittingly in order that we may fulfill that future; he looks after us carefully and follows everything we do, correcting our errors. And then . . . we are afraid of him.

It is worthwhile not to forget the *fiat* of our Lady; it was the answer of one creature to the *non serviam* of another creature. Such docility, and the fact of being completely, absolutely, and totally resigned to the will of God, on the part of the most humble, most pure, and perfect of creatures, opened the doors to the Son of God that he might save us. Who knows what may depend on the *fiat* that each of us gives to God's invitation!

It is not we who choose; it is God who chooses us: *Non vos me elegistis, sed ego elegi vos, et posui vos, ut eatis, et fructum afferatis,* "You have not chosen me; but I have chosen you; and have appointed you, that you should go and should bring forth fruit" (Jn 15: 16). It was not the Virgin who chose God, who chose to be the Mother of God; it was God who chose her for the divine maternity. In the same way, it is the Lord who chooses a mission for us, and chooses each of us for a determined specific task. We can see that vocation is not purely a matter of personal choice in the case of that man from Gerasa from whom Jesus had expelled a legion of demons: "Now the man from whom the demons had gone begged that he might be with him; but he sent him away, saying, 'Return to your home, and declare how much God has done for you.' And he went away, proclaiming throughout the whole city how much Jesus had done for him" (Lk 8: 38–39). He did not lack generosity, but that was not to be his way. His way was as the Lord indicated: to return to his home and to make known the miracles of God.

"To know as perfectly as possible the divine idea of holiness; to examine with the greatest care, so as to adapt ourselves to it, the plan traced out by God himself whereby we may attain to him: it is only at this price that our salvation and sanctification can be realized." [13]

This is logical. All the graces prepared by God for each of us, all the personal characteristics with which he has gifted us, all the personal circumstances that affect us one way or another, all these things come to us directly related to God's plan. If there are so many Christians who today live aimlessly, with little depth and hemmed in on all sides by narrow horizons, it is due, above all, to their lack of any clear idea of why they, personally, exist. They know in a general and very abstract way why they were created, but they are unable to connect this general idea with their own particular case. The connection between faith and life must be such that life is the result of faith; and what we usually refer to as supernatural outlook is what makes us relate everything we do, even the smallest thing, to God. "No, my children! We cannot lead a double life. We cannot have a split personality if we want to be Christians. There is only one life, made of flesh and spirit. And it is that life which has to become, in both body and soul, holy and filled with God: we discover the invisible God in the most visible and material things." [14] If such insistence on this matter of vocation seems excessive, it must be attributed to the basic importance that the question itself possesses. It is neither chance nor accident that the

[13] Blessed Columba Marmion: *Christ, the Life of the Soul,* I.

entire life of the Virgin Mary was a consequence of her maternity. What elevates a man and truly gives him a personality of his own is the consciousness of his own concrete task in the universe. It is this that fills a life and gives it meaning. Without this consciousness of vocation man tends merely to vegetate, and this is not proper to men made in the image and likeness of God.

[14] *Conversations*, no. 114.

2

THE VISITATION

In those days Mary arose and went with haste into the hill
country, to a city of Juda, and she entered the house of
Zachary and greeted Elizabeth. And when Elizabeth heard
the greeting of Mary, the babe leaped in her womb; and
Elizabeth was filled with the Holy Spirit and she exclaimed
with a loud cry, "Blessed are you among women and
blessed is the fruit of your womb. And why is this granted
me, that the mother of my Lord should come to me? For
behold, when the voice of yur greeting came to my ears,
the babe in my womb leaped for joy. And blessed is she
who believed that there would be a fulfilment of what was
spoken to her from the Lord." And Mary said, "My soul
magnifies the Lord, and my spirit rejoices in God my Savior, for he has regarded the low estate of his handmaiden.
For behold, henceforth all generations will call me blessed;
for he who is mighty has done great things for me, and
holy is his name. And his mercy is on those who fear him
from generation to generation. He has shown strength
with his arm, he has scattered the proud in the imagination
of their hearts. He has put down the mighty from their
thrones, and exalted those of low degree. He has filled the
hungry with good things, and the rich he has sent empty
away. He has helped his servant Israel, in remembrance of
his mercy, as he spoke to our fathers, to Abraham and to
his posterity for ever." And Mary remained with her about
three months, and returned to her home.

Lk 1: 39–56

Spirit of communication

The moment the Virgin Mary learned of the miracle of
Elizabeth's conception, she went to visit her. "In those days,"

says St. Luke, without further details. His mode of expression, however, seems to indicate not only that little time elapsed between the Annunciation and the Visitation, but that the one came immediately and as a consequence of the other. The words that the evangelist uses give the impression of haste; not the speed of traveling, but the quickness of something that one does immediately without postponing it to other things, the quickness of something that comes first and cannot be delayed; at the same time there is a notion of resolution and strength, as of someone who knows what she wants and where she is going, someone whose journey is the fulfillment of a duty; the word *exurgens* in Latin suggests not only rising but rising with decisiveness, and it is significant that the evangelist says that she went to the mountains of Juda *cum festinatione*, that is to say, with haste, with the rapidity of one who really wishes to arrive.

It was spring; perhaps the Paschal feast is near. The town, located in the south, in the mountains of Judea, is probably the present-day town of Ain-Karim. It took several—three or four—days to go from Nazareth to Ain-Karim, and it is probable that our Lady went with some of the caravans that were going to Jerusalem. It must have been a marvelous trip for her, just one of the crowd, alone with her joyful secret.

But why the hurry? Why this sudden journey? Quite sensibly, Maldonatus in his commentary on the Gospel of St. Luke rejects the opinion that this sudden trip was due to curiosity on the part of the Virgin to confirm what the angel had told her regarding her cousin. It is out of the question to think that she who had felt within herself the Incarnation of the Word would need to see with her own eyes the miraculous conception of Elizabeth. Without a doubt, the reasons that impelled her were, as St. Ambrose says, charity, humility, and spirit of God. Although this is true, it means little to the mentality of today, so we must try to go further, if we can, into the analysis of the mystery, in order to find the lesson it contains for us.

To begin with, it is evident that one should not disassociate this trip to Judea from the Annunciation. As we have already pointed out, the announcement of the conception of

John the Baptist does not seem to be a sign to help to sustain our Lady's faith; unlike Zachary she neither asked for, nor needed, a sign. Rather, it would seem to be a delicate way of letting her know that Elizabeth, through her son, was also connected with the great mystery of the Incarnation. The writer Franz Willam points out that the angel links the news concerning Elizabeth with the revelation made to Mary about the Incarnation of the Word by using the word "also" and that this indicates the relation between the two occurrences. This observation is probably correct.

One must remember that the Virgin Mary was not an angelic being but a human being, and that she was not exempt from the emotional reactions to which every human being is subject. It is easy to imagine her state of mind after the angel had left her: her soul overflowed with joy. But the intense joy that one feels at the beginning, quietly and alone, an interior joy in which all the faculties are concentrated on the happiness itself, a joy in which there is a large element of unspeakable gratitude, soon overflows and becomes a great exterior cheerfulness and gaiety. The Virgin must have experienced an immense gaiety above all because God's hour was at hand, because the Redeemer was already in the world. The longings that so many generations had felt over the centuries and through dire vicissitudes were at last fulfilled. God had given testimony of his faithfulness in fulfilling his promise, and the bridge between men and God, long destroyed by sin, was to be restored. A depressing nightmare was beginning to fade away, and humanity's guilt was going to be atoned for.

Added to that, the fact that she had been chosen! The Holy Spirit had overshadowed her, and the Messiah was engendered in her womb. And joy tends to communicate itself to others; it makes us laugh and smile, clap our hands and jump about; it is expansive and tends to overflow into others. Did not the woman who had found the groat she had lost run and share her joy with her neighbors (Lk 15: 8–9)? And the father of the prodigal son, when his son returned home, did he not order a huge celebration to be given in order that everyone might share his joy with him (Lk 15: 22)? Our

Lady was no different from us in this. She wanted to communicate her overflowing joy. But how and, above all, to whom?

The fact that St. Luke—and, indeed, all the evangelists—give so few of the inessential details forces us to supply a thousand small connections by our own efforts. But we must keep careful watch over our imagination; pure imagination is very capricious, and it is not our business to supply capriciously what Scripture does not tell us; rather, we must try to deepen our understanding of what has been revealed to us. The means at our disposal are study, reflection, meditation—and, above all, prayer after the manner of St. Thomas: that is, we must pray for better understanding. Knowledge, understanding of human nature and its essential and integral elements, all the advances of modern science, all these things are useful for they enrich the intelligence and make it more capable of achieving truth.

Obviously, we cannot know exactly what thoughts were provoked in the Virgin Mary by her new situation. We do know that joy is communicative. Always when we are overflowing with something we feel the need to communicate it to someone else. The angel's message was, first and foremost, a prodigious secret; the Virgin had not asked for any secret, but the news of this event which concerned her so intimately was revealed to her. She had no right to reveal the message, which had been confided in her, because after all, if God wanted others to know he could inform them in the same way as he had informed her. The very atmosphere of intimacy and solitude in which the Annunciation had taken place was an indication of God's will to keep it veiled in privacy. Consequently, she could share her happiness with no one, and even if she did share it, would it not thereupon become sorrow? Who would believe her? Who would even understand the miracle that had taken place in her, no matter how clearly she explained it?

God, however, had foreseen everything. Elizabeth was the person in whom she could trust, at least to the extent of rejoicing with her. Here perhaps we may be inclined to reason with an excessive amount of subtlety, but the Virgin's extreme delicacy may be said to pave the way for it. The only thing that Gabriel mentioned about Elizabeth was her fecundity. But the fact that he should mention her in the message at all was a sign that she was in some way connected with the message itself, that in some way the miraculous disappearance of her sterility was connected with the mystery of the Incarnation. The Virgin, then, found a way open to her to communicate her joy. Elizabeth's conception was a reason for rejoicing with her and at the same time a reason for the Virgin to give vent to her own happiness and speak about the wonders of God. Ultimately, the joy of the Virgin had a much larger measure of joy in God than mere self-satisfaction. Rather than communicate her secret, what our Lady really wanted was to show her happiness and gratitude. She felt like bursting into song in praise of God, who had been so immensely good to her. Apart from the impulses of the Holy Spirit, our Lady's journey to the house of Zachary and Elizabeth had a reason—or, at least a plausible explanation—in a deep human need: the need for communication.

Here again we find another point of contact between the Virgin's life and our own because we too, as human beings, feel this same strong impulse of nature. Did not St. Teresa of Avila, with her wide experience and her deep grasp of reality, say that everyone, however saintly, needs an outlet? The important thing, therefore, is to channel this need properly, because in this, as in everything else, deviation can be dangerous, not only on the supernatural level—where it causes more havoc—but even in one's human personality.

Man is a sociable being and cannot shut himself up completely with his own problems and preoccupations. The man who retires within himself—and here the expression must be taken in its literal sense and is not applicable to someone who is absorbed in speculations of a theoretical nature—is perverse and unadaptable. The spirit of communication, which puts us in contact with our neighbors, enriches us interiorly and makes us, as it were, more complete. And if one considers the matter in a negative sense, this unburdening is healthy, because there are some things within us which, if we do not expel them, become rotten. Freud owes his success largely to the fact that he hit the mark with what we might loosely call "lay confession," that is, to rid ourselves of whatever is troubling us internally, relieving the soul of a heavy burden.

Nevertheless, it is not so much a question of unburdening ourselves—which in any case becomes evident to anyone who thinks a little about it—as of proper channelling. The question, as we have seen in the case of our Lady, is: How, and to whom? For the most normal form in which the spirit of communication is manifested is not in our conversations with our neighbors or in our everyday dealings with others, for these are mere consequences of our social nature, but in that other more personal and more intimate relationship that we call confidence.

These intimate confidences with others solve the problem of how to give proper expression to this inner impulse of communicating something within us, be it happiness or sorrow. One does not confide in a crowd but in one person; and since confidence requires understanding, one does not confide in just anyone but in someone who deserves trust either because of what he is or because of the position in which God has placed him in relation to us. Any confidence demands a certain intimacy, and if this intimacy does not exist then the confidence creates it. Confidence requires that the person in whom we confide is able to understand the confidence completely. "The Christian apostolate—and I'm talking about an ordinary Christian living as just one more man or woman among equals—is a great work of teaching. Through real, personal, loyal friendship, you create in others a hunger for God and you help them to discover new horizons—naturally, simply. With the example of your faith lived to the full, with a loving word which is full of the force of divine truth." [1]

Confiding in someone else has reciprocal effects. When there is a "sharing," a sincere expression of true and intimate feelings, both parties receive something and grow interiorly—he who confides because, on giving expression to his

---

[1] J. Escrivá de Balaguer, *Christ Is Passing By*, no. 149.

happiness or sorrow, he frees himself from something oppressive, for happiness, too, can be oppressive; and he who is confided in because, being so trusted, he increases his sense of responsibility and frequently learns to rise above his own egotism in order to project himself into the happiness or sorrow of the other.

The most delicate point in this matter of confiding in another is the choice of a proper person. The Virgin Mary had no difficulty in choosing Elizabeth; and from the Gospel we get the impression of complete naturalness in the choice. Nevertheless, she acted with great discretion. Elizabeth was the only person whom she could choose for her confidence, for the simple reason that God himself, through the angel Gabriel, had chosen her. The Virgin did not allow herself to be led by her emotions, her feelings, or merely human judgment. If she did she would perhaps have chosen Joseph, that just man whom God had placed at her side. No, Mary was not guided by human judgment but by supernatural judgment, and we must never forget this. If we want to ask for advice about some practical matter or confide in someone about some purely human problem, it is enough to choose someone with intelligence, prudence, and discretion. But when it is a matter of the soul and the supernatural order, then one requires special sensitivity of spirit in order to know to whom God wants us to open our hearts. If we consider the matter from merely human motives, we run the risk of not being understood; and then our joy becomes bitterness, and the bitterness becomes misunderstanding. Then we feel uneasy; we feel uncomfortable because we have talked too much to the wrong person about the wrong matter.

It is good to confide our inner feelings if, like the Virgin Mary, we are discreet. In any of the details of our Lady's life which we find in the Gospel it is amazing to see how thoroughly she was filled with the Holy Spirit, how the only motivating force behind even the most insignificant of her actions was his grace. The choice of the person with whom she could share her joy was not a purely personal one because here too, as in the Annunciation, she limited herself to the acceptance of the will of God. And how difficult it is for man to limit himself, to know how to control his own initiative within the proper limits! The fact that Elizabeth was mentioned in the message implied that she was intimately connected with what was revealed in it.

This choice—or, rather, acceptance—of the person indicated to her for her confidence is something of the utmost importance. Given the need many of us have for opening our souls and exposing the most intimate and delicate feelings within us, the confidence brings out the most vital parts of our lives; and therefore, since understanding is essential, only someone who is spiritually fitted should share the intimacy of our soul. The parable of the Good Shepherd aptly illustrates what I am trying to express: only he who has a certain right—from God, of course—can enter through the door; the others are thieves and robbers, who bring ruin and have no care for the welfare of souls. "Allow me to give you a piece of advice. If ever you lose the clear light, always turn to the good shepherd. And who is the good shepherd? 'He who enters by the door' of faithfulness to the Church's doctrine and does not act like the hireling 'who sees the wolf coming and leaves the sheep and flees'; whereupon 'the wolf snatches them and scatters them.' Reflect on these divine words, which are not said in vain, and on the insistence of Christ who so affectionately speaks of shepherds and sheep, of sheepfold and flock, as a practical proof of the need that our soul has of good guidance." [2]

Anyone who seeks to penetrate into the intimacy of the soul with violence or cunning and with false motives—curiosity, desire to dominate, vanity, jealousy, or any other motive not based on a supernatural spirit—is a thief and a robber. Similar effects are produced when we are influenced by purely human motives—such as personal attraction—in choosing someone for our confidence, which then becomes a hindrance rather than a help. In other cases confidence can often become quite harmful. There is a kind of usurpation, and the result, instead of being joy and peace, is an

---

[2] *Christ Is Passing By*, no. 34.

uneasiness that frequently resembles the remorse of someone who has betrayed a secret that was not his to divulge.

The quality of the instrument

The first thing that Mary did when she arrived at Elizabeth's
house was something very simple and commonplace: she
greeted Elizabeth. It was the most natural thing she could
have done. Everybody does that on arriving at a house, but
nothing extraordinary ever happens as a result. One arrives
and one greets; the greeting is returned and conversation
begins.

The facts in that small town in the mountains of Judea,
however, did not exactly follow the normal pattern. The
moment Elizabeth heard the Virgin's voice, perhaps while
they were embracing and the usual words of greeting were
being exchanged: "Peace be with you," she experienced
something unusual and incredible, something that prevented her from answering the Virgin's greeting with the
customary promptness. Elizabeth, six months pregnant, unquestionably felt that her unborn child leapt with joy in her
womb.

The Precursor began his role as the herald of Jesus even
before he was born, giving testimony of Christ's presence in
the only manner that was possible for him, that is, by jump-
ing joyously in his mother's womb. Elizabeth felt herself
filled with the Holy Spirit and in that moment she understood everything. Had not Gabriel prophesied to Zachary
when he was announcing his conception and birth that he
would be full of the Holy Spirit "even from his mother's
womb" (Lk 1: 15). Elizabeth knew this, but she did not know
how or when it was to happen. At the very moment when
Mary greeted her and the child moved in her womb, the
Holy Spirit revealed to her the fullness of the mystery. In
that moment she understood everything: the joyful movement of her unborn child, the reason for her joy and the
deep and radiant happiness that suddenly overwhelmed her,
as well as the mystery that had taken place in her cousin.
"Blessed are you among women, and blessed is the fruit of

your womb!" she exclaimed, more as a result of her discovery than as an answer to Mary's greeting.

It all happened in a moment, in a few minutes at most, and was all a result of the simple fact that our Lady came and greeted her. But how is it that such a simple and everyday thing could bring about so many results? It is not too much to suppose that that was not the first time that the Virgin Mary had gone to the house of Zachary and had greeted Elizabeth; but nothing worth mentioning had ever happened before. At least we do not know, nor is it likely, that any other meeting between Mary and Elizabeth before the Incarnation had such importance.

The difference now was that our Lady was not alone; though she herself had not changed, she was not exactly as she had been at other times. The Blessed Virgin Mary was carrying in her womb the Word, the Son of God. God himself had taken possession of her being; next to the union of the three Divine Persons, there was no closer union than that between Mary and the Father, the Son, and the Holy Spirit.

The Virgin Mary greeted Elizabeth, and John the Baptist jumped for joy in his mother's womb. The next meeting between John and Jesus took place thirty years later on the banks of the Jordan, but then it was face to face, with no one between them. At the moment of the Visitation both Jesus and John were hidden; Mary and Elizabeth were between them like a double wall, and the Lord did not communicate with John directly but indirectly, through the presence of the Virgin and her voice. And John's mother also served as an intermediary. Elizabeth heard the greeting, and her son trembled with joy. It was as if a ray of sunlight passing through crystal fell upon a brilliant mirror and was reflected brightly upon another object. The Blessed Virgin was both the bearer of Christ and the instrument he used to sanctify John and fill Elizabeth with the Holy Spirit. Her physical presence and her voice were the instruments of grace. Our Lady was not like an opaque wall, which impedes the force of everything that takes place behind it, but, on the contrary, she was the means that allowed that force to have its full effect.

*   *   *

The phrase "to be an instrument" expresses just as well or even better than the word "creature" the relationship between Mary's entire life and God, and also the relationship that should exist between God and the life of each one of us. Everything in creation either is an instrument in the hands of God or else runs the imminent risk of remaining absolutely useless. It is possible that, because this concept of the creature being an instrument of God is not widespread, it has been scarcely developed in the ascetical field. Nevertheless, it expresses clearly our relationship with God, our function in the universe, the uniqueness and limitations of our particular mission in life. Here, as in so many other fields, the gradual separation that has come about between theology and thought, the excessive tendency to consider man in himself without reference to any other factors, has been extremely harmful, for it has left the way open to the idea that man is a completely independent being, whereas in reality he is independent only in a certain sense and up to a certain point. Humanism here performs a feeble service, for it darkens our vision and deprives man of the qualities that are essentially his, taking him out of the sphere in which he properly belongs and breaking his ties with everything that gives him consistency and makes him what he is.

We have already seen how important God's plan and vocation are for the existence of each of us. It is he who directs creation, who guides everything to the end which he himself has planned. This is the way things are, whether we like it or not, whether or not we admit it; it is an objective fact independent of all human opinion. Creatures are the means chosen by God to fulfil this end; they are his instruments. When the creature is made in God's own image and likeness, that is, when the creature is intelligent and free, this instrument must act in conformity with his own being: intelligently and freely. Then the creature is not a blind or mechanical instrument, and his actions take the form of collaboration. "Ever since I began to preach, I have warned people against a certain mistaken sense of holiness. Don't be afraid to know your real self. That's right, you are made of clay. Don't be worried. For you and I are sons of God—and that is the right way of being made divine. We are chosen by a divine calling from all eternity: 'The Father chose us in Christ before the foundation of the world, that we should be holy and blameless before him.' We belong especially to God, we are his instruments in spite of our great personal shortcomings. And we will be effective if we do not lose this awareness of our own weakness. Our temptations give us the measure of our own weakness." [3]

There are two conditions which, at least at first sight, are indispensable for an instrument to be truly useful: quality and docility. An instrument that lacks quality is useless because it is not adequate to fulfill the function for which it is intended. It is almost impossible to cut anything with a knife made of lead or cardboard or to paint any picture whatsoever, either good or bad, with a brush of wet clay. But an instrument of excellent quality that works by its own initiative is as useless as one of inadequate quality. To continue the metaphor, a knife of excellent steel, well-tempered and sharp, that is self-directed and allows no one to manage it would cut a great number of things that it should not cut. Not only would it be useless, but it would do much damage. A perfect brush that is not docile in the hands of the painter, however excellent it is, ruins the best canvas. Quality and docility are so necessary that we are useless and hopeless if we lack one or the other.

But what is quality? Of what does it consist and where does it reside in a person? Obviously, if we are to be instruments in the hands of God and collaborate with him we must have a certain minimum capacity, adequate quality, otherwise we run the risk of being a hindrance, of being something useless that no one can count on. Quality, then, is not so much a question of possibilities, of what a man might do, but of realities: what he really does at every moment, taking into account his development and the opportunities God offers him.

---

[3] *Christ Is Passing By*, no. 160.

Let us think for a moment about our Lord as he appears to us in the Gospels. He lived in the middle of the world, completely immersed in the life of his people and his time, allowing his life to unfold with complete naturalness. The activating principle in him was the Person, that is, the Word, the Divinity; but the Word acting in and through the human nature—body and soul—of Christ. And this humanity of nature was the instrumental principle the Second Person of the Trinity used as a means of manifesting himself. His voice and gestures, the imposition of his hands, his gaze, his expression and physical aspect, his loyalty and friendliness, his firmness and understanding, his human intelligence and the way he spoke: everything human in him was the instrument of his divinity.

Our quality, then, is based on our human personality and on all those natural talents and gifts that God has given us. It is God the Creator who has molded us, his creatures; he is the author of our personality and the shaper of our individuality. It is he who gave us a definite degree of intelligence and sensitivity; in the final analysis we owe him our senses, our knowledge; to him we owe our health and our peculiar capabilities, memory, will, physical constitution, and temperament. But for men, for beings made in the image and likeness of God, there must also be collaboration with God; God gifts us with certain qualities, but we ourselves must develop and perfect them. Even from a purely natural point of view this holds good. "The aim of life is self-development. To realize one's nature perfectly—that is what each of us is here for. People are afraid of themselves, nowadays. They have forgotten the highest of all duties, the duty that one owes to one's self. Of course they are charitable. They feed the hungry, and clothe the beggar. But their own souls starve, and are naked." These words, spoken by one of Oscar Wilde's more despicable characters,[4] show in a confused way what the Catholic Oscar Wilde thought deep within himself. This idea is true because, ultimately, personality is the faithfulness to a peculiar mode of being that God has given to each of us.

---

[4] *The Picture of Dorian Gray*, chap. 2.

And God does not want to do without us. His love makes him—forgive the expression—*need* us, need our poor and modest contribution in carrying out his work in each of us. God has given each of us certain qualities and talents at birth, and he leaves to ourselves the development and augmentation of these qualities. At the same time, however, if we so choose, God permits us to allow our gifts to fade away; he even lets us deform or misuse them. Many apparently normal Christians, many of those who scrupulously and habitually fulfill what are commonly called their "religious duties," are beneath it all deformed, twisted, mentally retarded or dwarfed, if we consider them from an overall point of view, both supernatural and human—the point of view of God. Sometimes they fail to cultivate magnificent qualities given to them by God in order to serve him and give him glory, and for lack of cultivation they have become stagnant; at other times, because of ignorance or negligence, obvious talents have not been developed to the full perfection that should have been expected.

This perfectioning of both the supernatural and human parts of our being, of our physical as well as our spiritual qualities, is indispensable for those who want to serve God in the way that he wishes to be served. Because of its importance to us, it would be well not to forget that the servant in the parable of the talents was thrown into exterior darkness because he was useless and lazy and had buried his talents instead of using them fruitfully (Mt 25: 30). It is true that (from a supernatural point of view) the molding of ourselves to be better instruments of God's will presents to us a vast battlefield for the ascetic struggle because it constantly imposes on us innumerable sacrifices and positive action that are genuine acts of mortification. Only in this way is it possible to fulfill the first of the requirements that the Lord asks of his servants, that they be *good* servants. "The price paid for each Christian is the redeeming Blood of our Lord, and he, I insist, wants us to be both very human and very divine, struggling each day to imitate him who is *perfectus Deus, perfectus homo.*" [5]

<hr>

[5] J. Escrivá de Balaguer, *Friends of God*, no. 75.

We may say then that the quality of our Lady was such that her voice was enough to awaken deep and wonderful feelings in a soul as sensitive to the supernatural as that of Elizabeth. The Lord never encountered the slightest obstacle in his Mother; on the contrary, he found in her such "transparency" that it was as if one could see him through her. There was nothing in the Virgin that could obscure or conceal her Son, nothing that could impede the complete manifestation of the Divinity that dwelt within her. Only the human nature of Jesus Christ, which was hypostatically united to the Word, surpassed Mary in quality.

The order established by God in the world is such that two souls never come in contact with each other as pure spirits. Each of them inhabits a body. In the world there are not souls but persons, and each person is a composite of soul and body. Ultimately, then, it is the human person on whom we must count to serve God, to reach sanctity. Grace does not destroy nature; it perfects it; it elevates nature to a supernatural level and purifies it of evil inclinations, of the blemishes and deformities and impurities with which original sin marked it. Consequently, the most developed personalities, the most mature and well-balanced, are the saints. It is not possible even to conceive a person who is not honorable on the human plane reaching perfection, supernatural sanctity; and even by stretching the imagination it is difficult to think of a coward, a cheat, a sluggard, a traitor, a liar, or a selfish person as an efficacious instrument of God's will. How is it possible for someone who is haughty and hard with his neighbors to have an interior delicacy for God?

Moreover, our Lady did scarcely anything out of the ordinary; she did only things that millions of people do every day; she visited the house of relatives: a greeting, a smile, a little favor. And why should she do more? It is very probable that oMoreover,oes not expect from us anything more than these little things; he does not expect amazing or extraordinary accomplishments but rather these menial daily tasks that *seem to be* monotonous, little things like a greeting or a visit. But if, like the Virgin Mary, we are bearers of Christ, and if as instruments we have the quality that the Lord expects of us, then it is almost inevitable that our very presence will speak of God. "Lord, how great you are, in everything. But you move me even more when you come down to our level, to follow us and to see us in the hustle and bustle of each day. Lord, grant us a childlike spirit, pure eyes and a clear head so that we may recognize you when you come without any outward sign of your glory."[6] It is pleasant to think that the arrival of Mary at Elizabeth's house brought with it a sweet sensation of happiness, a feeling of fulfillment and total peace. It is so beautiful to be sowers of peace and joy—the phrase is St. Josemaría Escrivá's—to spread the Christian way of life, that is, the spirit of Christ; and it is not only within our reach, but it is the first and most logical result of living as a Christian even in the most trivial of our daily actions; it is what our Lord asks of us, and it follows inevitably if we act in accordance with what we are. And in order to become less and less, as it were, opaque, in order that our nature may not obscure or deform the action of grace, in order to increase our aptitude for communication, it is necessary to cultivate the talents placed in us by God and thus to improve our quality.

The primacy of faith

In Elizabeth's reaction to the arrival of our Lady we find a progressive and gradual revelation of her feelings. After her initial surprise and delight on seeing her cousin, Elizabeth was astounded when she discovered the great mystery that had taken place in Mary, and she exclaimed: "Blessed art thou among women!" The Holy Spirit flooded her with light, for only in this way could she see what was hidden; no one else either learned of it or was able to guess its meaning because it could be understood only by supernatural means. Almost immediately we see the first result: Elizabeth was filled with admiration and gratitude for the honor that had been accorded her, for the woman who visited her was not simply Mary but "the Mother of my Lord," a fact manifested

[6] *Friends of God*, no. 313.

to her when she felt how John was sanctified in her womb. The same sentiment of humility, the same conviction with which the Blessed Virgin modestly expressed her dependency on God as his creature in her *Ecce ancilla Domini*, is also found, though in a lower degree, in Elizabeth's question: "And why is this granted me, that the mother of my Lord should come to me?" (Lk 1:43).

But we shall consider here not so much this sentiment of humility, which shows Elizabeth how unworthy she is of the honor done to her, as another affirmation of hers that is generally passed over, or at least not sufficiently stressed. This affirmation, in fact, is quite noteworthy.

When the Holy Spirit filled Elizabeth with this grace, he not only enabled her to understand the mystery of the Incarnation but also inspired her to reveal her innermost feelings, which are obviously genuine since they are the work of the Holy Spirit. Everything she said on that occasion bore the marks of being the fruits of that inspiration; as her feelings gradually manifested themselves in words, she climaxed it all with praise of Mary's faith.

Without doubt this is a fact worth noting. The first thing that usually comes to our mind when we think of the Virgin is her virginal purity, so delicate, or her amazing humility or her extreme and unsurpassed docility to God's plans or her faithfulness at the foot of the Cross. It is extraordinary that we should usually overlook Mary's faith when it was precisely her faith that the Holy Spirit inspired Elizabeth to praise above all her other virtues.

But even then the Holy Spirit did not go against her human nature or fail to take it into consideration. Elizabeth had a strong reason for noticing precisely the faith of our Lady because her husband Zachary had also received a message from the angel, the same Gabriel who had visited Mary, and had heard from his lips a message from God that fulfilled his fondest hopes. The angel had announced to Zachary that his wife Elizabeth was to conceive a son because his prayers had been heard. This revelation was addressed to Zachary because Elizabeth was not going to conceive through the power of the Holy Spirit, but through the act of man. But Zachary had not been as docile, as simple and trusting, as the Virgin Mary. He was, indeed, a pious man, a faithful servant, a just and God-fearing man, a man who had walked in God's presence *sine querela*, blamelessly (Lk 1:6), with a sincere desire of pleasing him. Zachary, too, on seeing the angel had been naturally shocked by such an extraordinary manifestation of the supernatural, and he was overcome with fear. But the angel said to him: "Fear not, Zachary, for thy prayer is heard; and thy wife Elizabeth shall bear thee a son" (Lk 1:13). Like Mary, the old priest had listened attentively, but he did not reflect interiorly, and his faith wavered. What the angel was telling him was so absurd! His wife Elizabeth was sterile, and both of them were quite old. How could such a thing be possible? Zachary was very old, knew life, had a wide experience, and was knowledgeable in many things! He was too old to become enthusiastic easily! He was not naïve enough to believe everything that people told him, even if it flattered him! Since he had been a young man he had been asking God for an heir, but to no avail, and now, when he was in his old age, with the vigor of his youth gone and the persistency of his prayer diminished, was his desire to be fulfilled? Perhaps Zachary was afraid of believing too much: he had wanted to have a son for so long that he was afraid of being disappointed again; perhaps in silence with Elizabeth during the best years of his life he had suffered the shame that accrued to them because of the sterility of their marriage; he did not want to suffer another disappointment now that he was resigned to his fate, now that his bitterness had finally given way to peace.

This pessimism that had nested in the noble and righteous heart of Zachary prevented him from clearly understanding supernatural things, and it was this pessimism that impelled him to ask for a confirmation, a palpable proof that what was being announced to him was true; he wanted a human testimony: "And Zachary said to the angel: How shall I know this? For I am an old man, and my wife is advanced in years" (Lk 1:18). The angel then forced him to believe it. Zachary asked for a proof and he got one; he was struck dumb until the fulfillment of everything that had been announced to him.

Although all these things were in Elizabeth's mind, when she praised her cousin's faith she was acting under an impulse of the Holy Spirit, who thus confirmed Mary's exceptional merit. It certainly is praiseworthy to believe something in spite of all the weight of human evidence being against it, in spite of the fact that it is outside all possible reasoning or even against the laws of nature. In the whole of Scripture until then, the most powerful act of faith is Abraham's, but even that pales beside the faith of the Virgin Mary.

Here the text of the original Greek differs slightly from the Vulgate. According to the Vulgate, the words of Elizabeth should be translated as follows: "Blessed art thou that hast believed, because those things shall be accomplished that were spoken to thee by the Lord" (Lk 1:45).

The Greek text says: "Blessed is the one who has believed that the things are going to be accomplished." The difference between the Latin and Greek translations is unimportant for us here, because the lesson of faith in both texts is the same.

It is not possible to get to the deepest roots of Mary's faith at the moment of the Annunciation. On the surface we get the impression that everything about Mary is easily explainable; but this impression is due in large measure to habit, for since our early childhood we have been familiar with the facts of Mary's life as the Gospels relate them. First of all, we must remember that the idea of motherhood was completely outside the Virgin's own prospect of her future. Among the Jews it was the custom for the women to marry young, and sterility was considered a great dishonor, a punishment from God, because if a woman did not give her husband children she eliminated all possibilities of being counted among the ancestors of the Messiah; furthermore, children were looked on as the fruit and the purpose of marriage, as the perpetuation of the house and the lineage, much more than they are nowadays. The total self-surrender to God, which Mary had made since she was a child, left her outside the Savior's ancestral tree. The message of the angel, therefore, broke her away suddenly and completely from everything that up to then had been the perspective of her future life; it opened up a horizon so vast and unimaginable, so far above everything human, that it was impossible for her to grasp it with reason alone.

Our Lady had no human guarantee that everything the angel told her would come true. That a woman should conceive without the cooperation of a man was something outside the laws of nature; that she should be the Mother of God was inconceivable. Everything that Gabriel told her exceeded enormously the everyday limits within which her life had progressed; not only that, but it went beyond all human limits. What was proposed—even more, *announced*—to her was something completely incomprehensible, and she could find nothing within herself to justify or explain the fact that such an announcement should be intended precisely for her. What was demanded of her was something of a truly superhuman grandeur, a limitless, absolute, and blind belief in the word of God, not only in relation to the Incarnation itself, but also in relation to everything that would derive from it. Considered from the human point of view, all that— even the presence of the angel--was absurd, a dream that fades along with the state of mind that causes it; it was something that, from a human standpoint, lacked logic and sense. Let us think of our own reaction to such a situation. Zachary, when faced with an infinitely lesser paradox, refused to believe; the thing seemed inconceivable to him. God did not permit the incredulity of a creature to disrupt his plans, and when Zachary asked for a sign, God gave it to him and forced him to believe.

But Mary was full of grace and the humblest of creatures. God asked more of her than he had asked of Abraham. She did not understand: the mystery remained a mystery; but she *believed* in God and in his omnipotence: she *knew* that he had revealed himself to her ancestors, and she *knew* his promises. She believed without hesitation what God communicated to her through Gabriel; she did not ask for visible signs, poor proofs for which we so often beg. In spite of the appearance of the angel, the acceptance of the message is a prodigious, inconceivably great act of faith. The Virgin trusted God and believed everything that he told her, and the Word was made flesh. The interior growth and the maturity that Mary underwent in that one instant are immeasurable; it is as if suddenly she were transported to a superior place, closer to God, with all the enlightenment and strength that such a transportation would imply; with all the feeling and profundity that one experiences after having penetrated through dense layers far into the center of things, where everything is found and everything is explained.

*   *   *

It is useless, when called to any vocation, to expect a concrete sign, visible proof on the human level, of the supernatural basis of the vocation. Faith is necessary in everything that concerns a superior world, the supernatural world. It is always possible, when we approach that delicate and narrow zone which divides the temporal from the eternal, nature from grace, the human from the supernatural, that doubt, not necessarily any serious objection, may begin to trouble us. There is an intimate relationship between humility and faith, between pride and scepticism. Ultimately the question is—at least, usually—settled not by dryly rational objectives but by grace.

Perhaps the parable of Dives and Lazarus will express more clearly what I mean. When Dives begs Abraham to send Lazarus to his father's house in order to warn his five brothers and give them a chance to change their evil ways and reform their lives, Abraham answers: "They have Moses and the Prophets, let them hear them." But he said: "No, father Abraham; but if some one goes to them from the dead, they will repent." And he said to him: "If they do not hear Moses and the Prophets, neither will they be convinced if someone should rise from the dead" (Lk 16: 29–31). The last words are conclusive. No argument can convince one who wants to doubt, one who refuses to believe even when there are enough, and more than enough, reasons for believing. Zachary asked for a sign; when he got it he believed: not everyone who asks for a sign and obtains one reacts in this way, for when one sees the message substantiated with the proof that one wanted, new doubts can easily arise and dispute its worth or its genuineness.

The primacy of faith, this extraordinary importance of believing in God, scarcely mentioned in Elizabeth's praise, is emphasized throughout all the Gospels. There are few points on which our Lord lays so much stress as on this point of faith. The continuous emphasis, often repeated and very serious, is contained in a whole multitude of evangelical texts so very straightforward and explicit that it is surprising how blind to them we Christians are. It was faith in Christ, that powerful weapon, which enabled a few common, poor, and ignorant men without friends or influence to change the whole face of the world. That was the only weapon the apostles had. All the preaching of St. Paul is centered on faith. He was not efficacious because of his learning or the eloquence of his words, but because he was a man who believed. St. John, with all his tenderness but also with firmness, declares: "For whatsever is born of God overcomes the world; and this is the victory that overcomes the world, our faith" (1 Jn 5:4). James the Less, in his Universal Epistle, speaks to us even more directly, as if he had a presentiment of the weakness of today: "But let him ask in faith [for wisdom], with no doubting. For he who doubts is like a wave of the sea that is driven and tossed by the wind" (Jas 1:6). "If you can believe," Jesus says to the father of the possessed boy, "all things are possible to him who believes" (Mk 9:22).

Such clear and explicit texts could be multiplied indefinitely. After the miracle of the loaves and fishes, the Jews who had witnessed it and had received the benefits of it asked Jesus: "What must we do, to be doing the works of God?" Jesus answered them, "This is the work of God, that you believe in him whom he has sent" (Jn 6:28–29). In spite of this constant stress on the part of Christ and his disciples, in spite of the fact that the fundamental condition for entering the Kingdom of Heaven is faith, today it is probably the virtue that is least practiced among Christians. Many of

them give the impression that they believe only theoretically, in one small isolated corner of their brain, without
anything which that faith implies having the slightest
influence on their everyday lives. A Christian's faith, the
faith of a disciple of Christ, should shape his whole mentality
and outlook, his ideas and principles of action, in theory and
in practice; but in many souls that faith lies dormant; it has
no influence either on ideas or on actions. It is because of
this lack of faith that there is such complete inconsistency in
the lives of Christians and in so-called Christian societies.
This inconsistency is like a deep chasm between two different worlds, a manifest and lamentable lack of unity in one's
life; it is as if a person's being were divided up into separate
compartments. It is in this sense that St. Josemaría Escrivá
writes: "The twin aspect of our objective—the ascetic and
apostolic—is so intrinsically and harmonically joined to and
integrated with the secular character of Opus Dei that it
brings forth a *unity* of life at once simple and strong—a unity
of ascetic, apostolic, and professional life—and turns our
whole existence into prayer, sacrifice, and service marked by
a filial way of dealing with the Most Holy Trinity."

The problem is plain to anyone who examines the question, and it is probably the gravest and most acute of all
the problems of our time. No one can live without believing
in something. The collective responsibility of Christians is
enormous: they have allowed ideologies to extinguish their
faith. The following testimony of a biologist whose investigations led him to the truth is extraordinarily explicit:
"We have preferred ... the lucubrations of the philosophic
thought of the eighteenth century. We have become stagnant in abstractions instead of advancing to concrete reality;
without any doubt concrete reality is difficult to grasp. And
our spirit prefers the least effort. Perhaps it is the innate
laziness of man which makes him choose the simplicity of
the abstract instead of the complexity of the concrete."[8] It is
true that the concepts enunciated by Adam Smith or Karl
Marx or the principles of the French Revolution carry much

---

[7] Letter, Rome, February 14, 1950, no. 5.

more weight than the words of the Gospel, even in the lives of many Christians. Our time is characterized, above all, by a tremendous crisis of faith, a humanization of the Gospel, a secularization of all revelation, of everything supernatural. We have been paying too much attention to those who base their ideas solely on their own authority; they have persuaded us that they were giving us living reality when, in fact, they were giving only dead ideas.

Man seeks security, but a security that he can control. Consequently, he lives faith badly, because faith implies a risk. What guarantee had our Lady that everything the angel announced to her was true and trustworthy and not a wild dream? But faith is not a consequence of reasoning; it belongs to a superior level; and in the same way as reason is an adequate instrument for natural things, faith is adequate for the supernatural and of its very nature needs the support of grace, because man of himself is unable to transcend his own limits. This implies a leap into what seems an empty darkness but is a reality full of light; it implies that we *believe* and *believe in* God, in spite of all the appearances of the physical world, in spite of all the artful reasons of a mind capable of error and weakened by original sin.

Again I refer to the words of our Lord to the Jews: "If any man's will is to do his will, he shall know whether the teaching is from God or whether I am speaking on my own authority" (Jn 7:17). We should note the relationship which these words establish between conduct and knowledge. Grace is increased in each of us and we draw closer to God in the same degree as that in which we wish to fulfill God's will, and it is by this disposition of the soul that we advance toward moral perfection. The closer we approach God, the more light there is, the more the clouds will disappear and knowledge becomes clearer and faith stronger and more vital; every effort we make, if properly directed toward the attainment of truth, perfects us morally. There is then an intimate and hidden relationship between the

---

[8] Alexis Carrel (1873–1944), French surgeon and biologist, 1912 Nobel prize winner, and author of several books reconciling mind and faith.

clarity of a mind enlightened by faith and moral rectitude, a relationship that especially affects metaphysical and supernatural truths. We cannot have for a revealed truth the same clear, cold, and objectively demonstrative evidence of a mathematical proposition; they belong to different spheres. If this were possible, there would be no need for faith, because that delicate equilibrium of the human balance between the divine weight and the human weight would be suddenly and irresistibly disturbed by the *pondus divinus*, the divine weight, and man would have no other choice but to accept passively the irrefutable proofs of things which would be completely within his own human limits: "If we could perceive that there is a God as clearly, as objectively, as we can demonstrate that two and two are four, then the divine 'weight' would weigh the scale to one side, and the physical 'weight' would be lifted up with a sudden jerk. Then we would no longer remain that delicate, human metaphysical scale whose two platforms are loaded with weights that either go up or down according to the way we succumb to evil or fight for good. There would be no room for that final decision which, in the interests of the development of his own personality, is left to the human being himself." [9]

This definite and ultimate margin of personal choice is the characteristic of faith; it is that which bestows upon it a special quality of an "intrepid struggle" and "bravery": "The meeting with God also bears the mark of bravery. It is true that whoever turns toward God has, thanks to the divine promises, the guarantee that God will receive him, but he does not know whom he is to face. God is shrouded in mystery and to his creatures he is the cause and object of the continual surprise." [10] The fact that we have to trust in the word of God, a hidden God, walking in darkness—for the clarity of the beatific vision will begin only after death— in the uncertainty of something that we can perceive but cannot touch, justifies Peter Wust's use of the reference to the bold "risk" of faith. Here all natural methods are useless.

[9] Peter Wust.
[10] Michael Schmaus.

It is like a leap taken blindfolded into the arms of God; for who ever trusted in God and was disappointed?

But there is a subtle step between knowing and believing, the step that separates knowledge from faith. It is like a child reading a book and understanding the individual words but being unable to grasp the meaning. Something more is needed: a certain inner ability to grasp at the heart of things, an ability that includes a supernatural faculty that does not depend on man but on God. To believe or not to believe does not depend, ultimately, on man, but on God. Nevertheless, in a certain sense one can say that faith does depend on man, because in principle God knows the capacity of each individual and he counts on that; only he whose will is disposed to believe will receive the gift of faith.

Faith, however, is not simply something to be contemplated. It is not merely a matter of giving assent to certain supernatural truths, trusting in God's word. Faith is something to be lived; we must let it penetrate our whole being and shape our entire life. Knowledge that is not lived, as has been said, is sterile. The just man—the Christian—must live by faith (Rom 1:17). The entire deposit of supernatural truths then ceases to be mere theory and becomes something of great force in our lives because it gives the believer a strength and audacity that nothing else could give him; then man finds the immovable pillar of support that gives him not only security but ability to carry out the greatest enterprises; then one can definitely speak of miracles and declare "We, too, would work them if we had enough faith." [11]

Pilate was a sceptical man. He did not believe in truth: "What is truth? " he asked (Jn 18:38). But, on the other hand, he believed in dreams. There are a lot of men who do not believe in grace but who do believe in science; who do not believe in sanctity but believe in progress and in happiness of mankind through the application of some political theory or another; who do not believe in God or in the Virgin or in dogmas but who raise to the level of indisputable

[11] J. Escrivá de Balaguer, *The Way*, no. 583.

dogma equality, fraternity, pacificism, and this or that economic doctrine. "They have no faith, but they do have superstitions. We laughed, and at the same time we're sorry, when that tough character became alarmed at the sight of a black cat or at hearing a certain word which of itself meant nothing but for him was a bad omen." [12] There are Christians who are passionately interested in certain political ideas, in business, or in some ideal, and who fight and suffer for these things, but remain indifferent, untouched by the only problems it is worthwhile being concerned about: grace and sin, faith and scepticism, the Church or sterile isolation, God or atheism. How applicable even today is Chesterton's thesis in *The Ball and the Cross*!

Only those live by faith who are willing to risk everything and trust boldly and courageously in God, with complete confidence in his word. They are like children. Faith does not admit of any reconsiderations: once a person takes the plunge toward God he must not turn back to consider himself or the circumstances around him. If he tries to turn back he runs the risk of sinking, a lesson that we can learn—if we want to—from the passage in the Gospel in which Christ goes to his disciples' boat walking on the water. Peter says to him: " 'Lord, if it is you, bid me come to you on the water.' And he said: 'Come' " (Mt 14: 28–29). And Peter, trusting in his word, jumps briskly out of the boat and walking on the water goes to meet him. But the moment Peter ceases to think only of Christ's words and begins to examine the human circumstances around him; when he ceases to be anchored to Christ's word and thinks of all the reasons which persuade him that to walk on the waters is simply impossible; when he thinks of the strong wind, the enormous waves: then he begins to sink. He calls to the Lord, asking for help; and Jesus, perhaps with a smile at seeing Peter so afraid, grasps him firmly and holds him saying: "O man of little faith, why did you doubt? " (Mt 14: 31). Whenever we think of human circumstances, of the obstacles, of the appearances, of reasons, instead of thinking only of the word

[12] *The Way*, no. 587.

of God, of revelation, of the impulse of the Holy Spirit, of the interior voice of grace, then we begin to sink. He who hesitates certainly sinks. That is why in matters of "faith, purity, and vocation" there can never be any arguing with temptation, says St. Josemaría Escrivá. If we argue in these matters we sink, because we give more authority to the natural than to the supernatural.

If our Lady had thought of the madness of what was being suggested to her, of the risk it implied, of the impossibility of being both virgin and mother, of her own unworthiness, of the impossibility of conceiving through the power of God and that her son should be the son of God; if she had stopped to think of all these things she would never have believed, and none of the angel's message would have been fulfilled. Instead she thought and reflected that God is omnipotent; she thought of the promise made to Abraham, of the words of the prophets revealing the message of God; she remembered that she was a creature—and she pronounced her *fiat*, and the Word was made flesh. She was capable of believing and everything was realized, because "with God nothing will be impossible" (Lk 1: 37). Faith is the collaboration of man in the exercise of God's power.

We, with our too earthly view of the things of the spirit, have settled down comfortably to a faith more theoretical than alive, a faith that is more routine and habitual than doctrinal and based on conviction; we rest in our faith without fatigue, but without any vitality. Faith, as the Church teaches us and Christ demands from us, is the most vital and efficacious, the decisive thing, in the existence of every Christian.

"If you can believe, all things are possible to him who believes," Jesus warns the father of the poor sick boy (Mk 9: 23). Faith puts the power of God at our disposal, and also it puts us and and everything we possess at God's disposal.

Humility and docility

It is easy to understand Mary's reaction to the testimony given to her mission by the Holy Spirit, through Elizabeth.

Mary, without uttering a word, without in any way betraying the fact that she possessed a great secret, witnessed to Elizabeth's greeting, which was like a confirmation of the words of the angel, a confirmation she neither asked for nor wished, but which she received with great joy. She rejoiced because it came from God, and also because it implied a recognition of the great message on the part of God's creatures. Up to that point the revelation, as far as humanity was concerned, was known only to the Virgin herself, who was the principal person involved in the event, the protagonist, the subject in whom all the revelation was to be fulfilled. Now that limit was extended to Elizabeth. It is as if the Virgin had been the subject of a double revelation, as if God—in order that the two levels of existence might participate in it—wished to communicate his plans by means of the superior or supernatural world, the angel, and also of the lower or natural world, Elizabeth, thus bestowing blessings on her from all sides: "For to everyone who has will more be given, and he will have abundance (Mt 25: 29)." Mary had sufficient faith, and she neither needed nor asked for proofs, but God, who never lets himself be surpassed in generosity, gave her a conclusive proof by using one of his creatures to confirm the miracle taking place in her.

Full of happiness, transported by joy, the Virgin burst into song. The Magnificat is a spontaneous and poetic manifestation of the interior feelings that filled her and also an expression of the innermost core of her being and her relations with God. It is really amazing to see the simplicity and the facility with which our Lady does and says these things which, when we consider them more closely, we find are complex and difficult from our level of understanding; how quickly she penetrates to the very bottom of things.

She also was inspired by the Holy Spirit to give expression to her exaltation. Most of the verses of the *Magnificat* are taken from Scripture, mainly from the Psalms, and our Lady herself added very little. As Elizabeth, inspired by the Holy Spirit, praises her cousin's faith, Mary answers with a joyful song in praise of humility. The *Magnificat* is above all a wonderful praise of Almighty God, an act of thanksgiving for the goodness of the Creator. To be sure, the Virgin Mary speaks of herself, and in terms that may at first surprise us: "For, behold, henceforth all generations will call me blessed" (Lk 1:48). On her own initiative she would never have said such a thing, nor would such an outlandish thought ever have occurred to her. Who would think that a little, unknown country girl from Palestine, with no great future to look forward to, would solemnly proclaim that she was to be remembered by all future generations until the end of the world? How could she see into the future? But the Holy Spirit is God, and God does see into the future, and it was he who inspired her to make such a declaration, just as it was he who gave her justifiable motives for making it.

In the *Magnificat* the Virgin makes a clear distinction between Creator and creature, God and herself. All generations will call her blessed because "he who is mighty has done great things for me" (Lk 1:49). She does not find in herself anything that deserves praise or merits being remembered until the end of time; and she cannot find in herself the reason why God performed such great things in her; the only reason she can find for God's having so favored her is because "he has regarded the low estate of his handmaiden" (Lk 1:48). She acknowledges that she is nothing more than a handmaid of the Lord, the *ancilla Domini*, whose only distinction in the eyes of the Creator is her humility, her lowliness, her insignificance, her nothingness, her helplessness, her weakness—the fact that she is a creature dependent on God with nothing that God has not given her. The *Magnificat* is also an acknowledgement of grace; she has not done anything; it is God who has done great things to her, because he has regarded her lowliness.

It is difficult to express adequately in common language the profundity of this distinction made by the Virgin between Creator and creature. In the Virgin's words there is a kind of surprise, an amazement before the mystery of God's free choice, a clear consciousness, a terrifying consciousness of the absolute and immeasurable disproportion between the miracles God had worked in her and what she herself was; she expresses an overwhelming sensation of her own insignificance before the power and goodness of the Father. An irrepressible torrent of thankfulness springs from the depths of our Lady's soul and overflows into spontaneous expression, interlacing her song with verses from Scripture that in the past served her people to praise and give thanks to God. She stresses the suggestion that she owes everything to God, that everything is given freely to her as a gift, a gift freely given for no other reason than that God so wished.

Elizabeth exulted her faith, but Mary sang a canticle in praise of humility. The first impression that one gets on reading the *Magnificat* is that everything it contains is true; its truth is quite obvious. It is only just that she should give thanks to God, because he had done great things for her. Why should Mary have been chosen from among millions of women to be the mother of the Messiah, full of grace? It had never even occurred to her that she might be counted among the ancestors of the God made man, and she was unable to understand the mystery fully, although she knew what the mystery was. She had not willed herself into exist-ence, or chosen to be a woman, or chosen the race to which she would belong. God had arranged everything according to his own will and she, seeing this clearly, could hardly find words to show the extent of her thankfulness: she had to take them from Scripture. Her thankfulness was justified; it was true that God had done great things, and and it was her duty to recognize this and be thankful for it.

It is very difficult to define humility, but perhaps if we examine the words of our Lady and their deep significance, we may—within the limits of our understanding—be able to deduce some fundamental elements. There are two special traits, two great coordinates, as it were, that immediately strike us in the *Magnificat*: first, acknowledgement of a truth, of a fact, namely, that God had done great things to her; and second, thankfulness for the gift, for the grace, implied in the truth. That is to say, there is first of all an attitude of mind and then an act of the will derived from this attitude. The will is moved by the intelligence; thus we can see that, in regard to humility, the first and most important thing, the thing we may call the essence of humility, is that it must be based on truth. That is precisely the definition given by St. Teresa: "Once when I was thinking about why our Lord attached so much importance to humility, I immediately saw that this is so because God is All Truth and humility is walking in the truth; it is a fact that nothing good comes from us, only misery and nothingness; whoever does not understand this walks in lies. The one who understands this best walks in truth and pleases God who is All Truth." But there is an even higher authority than St. Teresa. Christ defined himself on a certain occasion as "the way, and the *truth*, and the life" (Jn 14:6), and on another occasion he said: "Learn from me, for I am meek and *humble* of heart" (Mt 11:29). Thus the Lord is humble; there is, consequently, an essential relationship—of essence—between truth and humility. This relationship can be put to the test. If the essential relationship between humility and truth that has been demonstrated does exist, then there must be a similar relationship between their respective opposites: pride and falsehood. If we say that humility is truth—which is correct—then it must be also correct to say—as it is—that pride is falsehood. We know from theology that the devil is characterized, above all other distinctive characteristics, by pride. It was pride that gave him his demoniac mark, that transformed him from an angel full of grace to an angel full of sin. There is a passage in St. John that describes a discussion between our Lord and the Pharisees, one of the most heated and violent discussions our Lord ever had, in the course of which Christ says: "You are of *your* father the devil. . . . He was a murderer from the beginning, and has nothing to do with *the truth*, because there is *no truth in him*. When he speaks a lie, he speaks of his own; *for he is a liar, and the father of lies*" (Jn 8:44). There is, then, a strange and mysterious relationship between lying and pride, and both—which are fundamentally the same thing—are related to injustice, in the same way that humility and truth are directly related with a sense of justice.

One must realize that humility is not a negative virtue. Not only does it deny, but it affirms, for truth is never a negation. Thus, there arises a subtle falsity when, under the appearances of humility, one denies what is evident and true.

It is not humility to believe God does not give us gifts: "Let us understand it perfectly, as it is, that God gives them to us without our meriting them, and let us give thanks to God for this. Otherwise, we frighten the soul into thinking that it is not capable of receiving great gifts if, when God begins to give them, the soul begins to tremble in fear of becoming proud" (St. Teresa).

It is evident that the essence of humility does not consist in despising oneself. No one could imagine for a moment that the Virgin Mary ever despised herself. Christ himself was humble, and how could he have despised himself? Self-contempt is, at best, a consequence; it is an impulse of the heart stemming from acknowledgement of the truth that we are sinners, capable of any treachery, of any bitterness, of any baseness, of everything that is low and contemptible, if God does not sustain us by his grace.

It is extremely important to remember that humility is truth; a man is humble to the same degree that he is truthful, to the same degree that he *sees* the truth. Again it is necessary to insist on the subtle difference, already noted, between understanding and seeing. For instance, we could *understand* perfectly the argument of a mathematical proposition and still not be able to *see* it. Everyone understands that he is a creature and, however little he thinks, he also understands the consequences that follow. Nevertheless, those who can fathom the tremendous depths of this truth are very few. One can have eyes and not see, ears and not hear, intelligence and not be able to reason correctly; for there is also a close relationship between humility and sight, between pride and blindness.

The man who is humble sees. There are certain things that are revealed only to children and to those who are like children, things that are hidden from the wise men of this world. Pride destroys in man the capacity to see ultimate realities, realities of the supernatural world which, because of their depth, require great penetration. Pride distorts reality because, seen through a veil, reality becomes deformed and blurred. Pride makes us lose all sense of proportion, because it completely disrupts our sense of measure and distance. The tree in the wood that is nearest to us may seem the biggest, but that does not mean that it is the biggest, something that a normal person realizes perfectly. If one acts according to what seems and not according to what is, one gets involved in all kinds of absurdities.

It is a very old problem. St. Paul, during the clash between Christianity and the pagan world, saw very vividly the monstrosities produced by pride—that is, blindness—in these haughty sages of the ancient world. The words in which he describes this phenomenon, although written centuries ago, are still applicable today.

"For the wrath of God is revealed from heaven against all ungodliness and wickedness of men who by their wickedness suppress the truth. For what can be known about God is plain to them, because God has shown it to them. Ever since the creation of the world his invisible nature, namely, his eternal power and deity, has been clearly perceived in the things that have been made. So they are without excuse; for although they knew God they did not honor him as God or give thanks to him, but they became futile in their thinking and their senseless minds were darkened. Claiming to be wise, they became fools, and exchanged the glory of the immortal God for images resembling mortal man or birds or animals or reptiles. Therefore God gave them up in the lusts of their hearts to impurity, to the dishonoring of their bodies among themselves, because they exchanged the truth about God for a lie and worshiped and served the creature rather than the Creator, who is blessed for ever! Amen. For this reason, God gave them up to dishonorable passions. Their women have changed natural relations for unnatural, and the men likewise gave up natural relations with women and were consumed with passion for one another, men committing shameless acts with men and receiving in their own persons the due penalty for their error. And, since they did not see fit to acknowledge God, God gave them up to a base mind and to improper conduct. They were filled with all manner of wickedness, evil, covetousness, malice. Full of envy, murder, strife, deceit, malignity, they are gossips, slanderers, haters of God, insolent, haughty, boastful, inventors of evil, disobedient to parents, foolish, faithless, heartless, ruthless" (Rom 1: 18–31).

The man who believes he is capable of doing something alone and unaided is simply a monster blinded by pride, unjust with God. He is blind: he does not see that in order to live from minute to minute, in order to breathe, to move, to think, he needs action on the part of God; he does not see that he would return to nothingness if God did not maintain him in existence every second. Eugene Boylan explains that we are like the sound of a man's voice: if he stops speaking, the sound ceases to exist. He also fails to *see* the defect left in him by original sin, with his understanding subject to error, with his will at the mercy of every impulse. He does not see his own essential instability, his impotence, his freedom enslaved by sin. He relies on himself, on his own intelligence, on his own ability, his own strength, his own power, his own talents, as if he had given these things to himself, as if he were not indebted to anyone for them. The proud man, in this also, is essentially unjust. Such a man thanks no one, withholding what belongs to another, refusing to give God what is his: "Or what hast thou that thou hast not received? And, if thou hast received, why dost thou glory, as if thou hadst not received it?" Since pride blinds one, the proud man is unable to see his own weakness; he has a completely false idea of himself and he believes he is self-sufficient; since he thinks thus he feels he does not need God, and he does not ask him for help. He is like a man who starves himself. His weakness increases, and finally he falls into the deepest abysses, trying to justify himself, but never recognizing his own misery, treating as truth what in fact are lies, treating as merit what is really shame, treating as virtue what is downright vice, denying sin and ignoring grace. Thus the proud man makes himself the measure of all things; he tries to make himself a superman but ends up lower than any man, almost reduced to the irrationality of an animal. Humanly he does not know himself because he ignores, on principle, what he is in essence: the image and likeness of God.

It has been repeated endlessly—and *The Way*, no. 609, reminds us of it—that "self-knowledge leads us by the hand, as it were, to humility." But we must not think that this exercise of self-knowledge is limited to philosophical reflection on our own ego. A woman with little formal learning, but with a deep wisdom derived precisely from her humility, settles this point: ". . . in my opinion, we can never completely know ourselves without knowing God; looking at his grandeur, let us consider our own lowliness" (St. Teresa). Lowliness is a relative concept; one's height is determined in relation to something or someone that serves as a comparison. In the *Magnificat* there is a constant reference from God to creatures and from creatures to God, a chain of contrasts, a continuous coming and going from greatness to lowliness and from lowliness to greatness. Gradually the attention is focused little by little on the greatness of God, more and more intensely and more permanently, until eventually one reaches the most perfect expression of humility: forgetting oneself and depending completely on God, a dependence that makes us want to disappear so that God may appear, to renounce all glory in order that only God may be glorified.

Now we come to the second integral element of humility. The first, as we have seen, is the attitude of mind, the grasp of truth. Now we must see how that attitude is to be expressed. The first element belonged to the intelligence, the second is the action of the will. There is a word which defines this second element, this *expression* of the attitude of mind: the word *submission*, or, if you like, *docility*.

In *The Diary Of A Country Priest*, the old and stalwart priest of Torcy says the following to his young colleague: "Miracles are the pictures—the pretty pictures in the book. But remember this, lad, our Lady knew neither triumph nor miracle. Her Son preserved her from the least tip-touch of the savage wing of human glory. No one has ever lived, suffered, died in such simplicity, in such deep ignorance of her own dignity, a dignity crowning her above angels. For she was *born* without sin—in what amazing isolation! A pool so clear, so pure, that even her own image—created only for the sacred joy of the Father—was not to be reflected" (Georges Bernanos).

She knew nothing of her own dignity. Because of this, in

her own eyes, she had not the slightest importance. She never depended on herself; she depended entirely on God, on his will. Thus she was able to judge the extent of her own lowliness, and to understand her own helpless but, nevertheless, secure condition as a creature: feeling herself incapable of anything and sustained only by the goodness of God. As a result of this selflessness she surrendered herself completely to God and lived solely for him.

As already mentioned, the second condition for being an efficacious instrument of God is docility. Only the humble can be docile. Those who lack humility follow the dictates of their own will, relying on their own ability; they have faith in themselves; they act on their own initiative because they believe they are self-sufficient; and they trust their own judgment; thus they can do great harm because they put last things first, and, instead of building, they destroy. They do not adapt themselves to God's plan—if they know it—because they will not tolerate being relegated to positions inferior to those they think they deserve. They forget these words: "Whoever would be great among you must be your servant, and whoever would be first among you must be your slave" (Mt 20: 26–27). Their ego is so strong that it leaves no room for anything else, not even for grace, and considers only itself. Those who lack humility, instead of occupying the place designated for them by God and fulfilling their function, and thus helping others to occupy their respective places properly and grow closer to God, disturb the divine action by getting out of place, seeking only their own glory and personal vanity. And in the Mystical Body of Christ this is very serious: as if some important organ of the body, instead of fulfilling its own function in relation to the rest of the organism, were to develop disproportionately at the expense of the rest. This may easily hurt other members, deforming them, diminishing them, atrophying them, retarding their development, making them do the work intended for itself but which it neglects in its efforts to outgrow all the others. It is like a corroding cancer.

Just as there is a deformation of humility that concerns

the intelligence, rejecting the true, objective progress of the soul through the action of God, there is another characteristic deformation that concerns the will: conventionalism in conduct. This defect stems from a divorce between thought and life. In other words, it is based on the belief that humility consists of acts when, in reality, humility is reflected in acts, creating and shaping them. This deformity always ends in a splitting of the personality, in hypocrisy, and, consequently, in falsehood and pride. "Naturalness and simplicity are two marvelous human virtues which enable men to take in the message of Christ. On the other hand, all that is tangled and complicated, the twisting and turning about one's own problems—all this builds up a barrier which often prevents people from hearing our Lord's voice." [13] This false humility is the exact opposite of spontaneity and is far from being an expression of truth. Those who always speak badly of themselves, keeping their eyes to the ground, those who are shy, those who are cowards, those who do not stand up for their rights (remember St. Paul's declaration of Roman citizenship, Acts 22:25–29), those who cover themselves with insults and defamations—how often we are insulted when others tell us we are what we say we are—and manifest many other like traits of conduct, all those people are not humble and have nothing to do with humility; all their acts are mere theatricalism. There is a dissociation between their inner being and the external surface, the face they show the world, which never expresses their real convictions, but from the very beginning is severed from their inner self and owes its origin to purely artificial calculation, since it pays attention only to appearances, to exterior behavior, but leaves untouched the depths of their being, the source of all activity. This is hypocrisy, the basic sin of the Pharisees.

God replies to the attitude that each person adopts to him, and the reply depends directly on the attitude and is provoked by it. The second part of the *Magnificat* refers to this clearly: "He has shown might in his arm, he has scattered the proud in the imagination of their hearts, he has put

---

[13] *Friends of God*, no. 90.

down the mighty from their thrones and has exalted those of low degree. He has filled the hungry with good things, and the rich he has sent empty away" (Lk 1:51–53). God is attracted by the humble and repelled by the proud. Whoever is emptied of himself is capable of being filled completely by God; but whoever lives for himself and is filled with his own ego has no room for God; God cannot fill him because he is already full. When St. James the apostle says: "God opposes the proud, but gives grace to the humble" (Jas 4:6), he expresses that incompatibility which exists between God and the proud. The point of contact between God and man is grace; and grace can enter only where there is room for it and where it is invited.

Taking into account what has already been said about humility, we can draw one or two conclusions. Since, as we have seen, faith is ultimately a grace, a gratuitous gift, something freely extended to us by God, it is evident that faith will be in direct proportion to humility. A humble man without faith, but who sincerely desires to have faith, will certainly end up by receiving the gift, because God refuses no one. On the other hand, the more pride increases, the more faith diminishes. The man who is humble and clearly realizes what it means to be a creature weakened by original sin does not rely on himself, does not trust himself; and the more clearly he sees how untrustworthy he is, the more he relies on revelation. The most humble of all creatures, our Lady, immediately believed the message of the angel. The fact that it is difficult to *see* the will of God in matters of vocation is frequently due to a hidden pride that weakens a man's faith and prevents him from taking the risk. I refer again to vocation because, after all, it is the keystone to everyone's existence.

From all this we may deduce the enormous importance of the virtue of humility: "It is the virtue which helps us to recognize, at one and the same time, both our wretchedness and our greatness." [14] There is no spiritual book, no saint, that has not stressed the extreme importance of humility,

[14] *Friends of God*, no. 94.

since it is the magnet that irresistibly attracts God. It is imperative, then, to acquire humility. But how?

Perhaps the simplest way to learn to be humble is the same way as one learns to walk. Children learn to walk simply . . . by walking. Since humility is truth, we will be humble according as we are truthful and the surest way—perhaps the shortest and fastest way—is to be sincere. Sincerity is a subject discussed rather infrequently, but, nevertheless, we must say something of it here. To be sincere means always to tell the truth; not only the truth, but the *whole* truth. This is very difficult at times, and often needs bravery and courage bordering on heroism. This is no exaggeration. Sincerity often makes us reveal many little things about ourselves that often make us more ashamed than bigger but less intimate matters. We must be sincere, above all, with God; but also with ourselves, in the depths of our own conscience. There is a very human tendency in all of us—too exclusively human to be completely good—to make a good impression and not a bad impression. That is why we are so clever at inventing excuses, justifications, explanations, mitigations. "You never want 'to get to the bottom of things.' At times, because of politeness. . . . But always because of fear! "[15] Most of the time we lie because of the fear of being caught in something not quite perfect, to hide the things that make us ashamed or embarrassed or that might provoke criticism from others. Since lying is a direct attack on humility because it causes a falsification of truth deep within us, only a ruthless sincerity, without fear of anyone or anything, can lead us directly to true humility. It does not matter that we cannot always keep up appearances; after all, we are what we are, and it is foolish to try to fool anyone. What is important is that God should be satisfied with us and that we remain on good terms with him. As already mentioned, there is an intimate connection between the concepts of humility and justice. No one has the right to keep what is not his; and if with an excuse, with a cunning explanation, we hide what should be revealed, we

---

[15] *The Way*, no. 33.

may appear good in the eyes of men, but we have still kept something that is not ours, that we do not deserve; we have been unjust. "Take truthfulness, a virtue so clean and pure. Can it be true that it has fallen into disuse? Has the practice of compromise, of "sugar-coating the pill" and "putting on a show," finally triumphed? People are afraid of the truth, and to justify their attitude they make the shabby excuse that no one practices or tells the truth anymore, that everyone has to resort to pretense and lies." [16]

It is not men but God who will judge us. How easy it is, however, for subtle temptations to spring from the depths of our nature, to smooth over what is rough. We have a strange tendency not to admit with any clarity the things that displease us. The man who is not sincere is like a sick man who is developing cancer and says nothing about it, trying to convince himself that there is nothing wrong with him. At times it is a mere insignificant detail that tinges our acts; nothing to worry about, we think. It may be, but the sooner we accept and recognize it the better. The harder a thing is to say, the more determined we should be to reveal it—to the right person, of course: God, ourselves, our confessor or spiritual director. Remember what we said about confidences.

Then we will really begin to know ourselves and to see the unfathomable capacity we have for evil. Then, when we turn our sins over and over in our minds, like dirty clothes pulled out of the bottom of our souls to be thrown away, we realize how few motives we have for being vain: what would happen if the rest of the world knew what we and God know about ourselves!

Of all the human virtues, sincerity is clearly the most important and the one that requires most attention. It is so important because, from its very essence, it leads directly to the supernatural virtue of humility, and humility is the necessary and indispensable foundation for all interior growth, since this growth is the work of grace. God did great things to the Virgin Mary because he saw the humility of his

[16] *Friends of God*, no. 82.

handmaid. He will hardly do great things in us if he does not find us also humble. "Let us turn our eyes toward Mary. No creature ever surrendered herself to the plans of God more humbly than she. The humility of the *ancilla Domini* ('the handmaid of the Lord') is the reason we invoke her as *causa nostrae laetitiae* ('cause of our joy'). After Eve had sinned through her foolish desire to be equal to God, she hid herself from the Lord and was ashamed: she was sad. Mary, in confessing herself the handmaid of the Lord, becomes the Mother of the Divine Word, and is filled with joy. May the rejoicing that is hers, the joy of our good Mother, spread to all of us, so that with it we may go out to greet her, our Holy Mother Mary, and thus become more like Christ, her Son." [17]

---

[17] *Friends of God*, no. 109.

3

IN THE TEMPLE

Now his parents went to Jerusalem every year at the feast of the Passover. And when he was twelve years old, they went up according to custom; and when the feast was ended, as they were returning, the boy Jesus stayed behind in Jerusalem. And his parents did not know it, but supposing him to be in the company they went a day's journey, and they sought him among their kinsfolk and acquaintances; and when they did not find him, they returned to Jerusalem, seeking him. After three days they found him in the temple, sitting among the teachers, listening to them and asking them questions; and all who heard him were amazed at his understanding and his answers. And when they saw him they were astonished; and his mother said to him, "Son, why have you treated us so? Behold, your father and I have been looking for you anxiously." And he said to them: "How is it that you sought me? Did you not know that I must be in my Father's house?" And they did not understand the saying which he spoke to them.

LUKE 2:41–50

The conduct of Jesus

Without doubt, these verses of St. Luke contain one of the more disconcerting episodes in the life of our Lord.

Every year the Israelites had to go to Jerusalem. Mary and Joseph used to go, of course, and when the child grew up and was old enough to go too, they took him with them. Generally the trip was made in a large group because there was always a great number of people going to the Temple during Passover to worship God. The children were not confined to any one group among the crowds of men and women but went where they liked, running along the road from one group to another. The custom was to agree on the meeting place, the time of departure, and the place they would meet at the end of the day's journey, when the various families gathered together to rest.

The day that Mary and Joseph ended their stay in Jerusalem and started on their way home they were not worried when they missed Jesus because they assumed he was with one of the other groups in their caravan. He could have been in any part of the caravan, with the other children in any of the groups or families. Although at first they were not concerned, gradually they became uneasy when he did not appear, and they went looking for him from one group to another among their relatives and friends. At sunset when the caravan stopped and the families gathered together, it became evident that Jesus was absent. That same night they returned to Jerusalem. They asked everyone who knew him, they inquired in all the places where he could be, they spent a whole day of anxiety and tension looking for him, but in vain. Then another troubled and sleepless night, of worry and torture and terrible fears. Where could he be? What had become of him? What could have happened so suddenly, so unexpectedly? On the third day, at last they found him: he was in the Temple, "sitting among the teachers."

Mary's first reaction was undoubtedly one of joy. A sensation of immense relief ended the anguish and anxiety of the previous days. Undoubtedly, too, she was surprised at the ease with which he conversed with the teachers, asking questions and answering in his turn with complete confidence—and at the effect that the profundity and prudence of his words had on them, as well as their approving gestures of astonishment and admiration. It certainly was an unexpected spectacle. St. Luke himself notes the surprise that Jesus aroused in his parents when they found him: "And when they saw him, they were astonished." It was not long, however, before astonishment gave way to a new feeling. Looking at Jesus, as serene as if this were where he really belonged, seated listening to the teachers of Israel, carefully attending to their explanations, asking questions and completely immersed, absorbed by the discussion, our Lady felt that same anxiety stir up within her again even more strongly than when she had first missed him. She had been suffering greatly because of his absence, but Jesus gave no sign of having suffered because of this separation from his parents. On the contrary, it seemed that he had not worried about them in the least. He did not give the impression that he had bothered to look for them or to let them know where he was. And there he had been, safe and sound all the while. Why had he not told someone what he intended to do? Why did he not tell anyone where he was? Why had none of the people they asked known something about him? He must have done this on purpose: he had told no one he was lost, and, even worse, he seemed to find his new situation quite pleasant. After all, he was twelve years old, and if he had wished he could have done something to let his parents know where he was. Had he, in fact, forgotten them? Was such a thing possible? Is it possible that he did not consider the worries and anxieties his parents would suffer when they missed him.? How can we explain the fact that Jesus, who was so docile, so obedient, so good, could be so unconcerned about his parents?

The Blessed Virgin, disturbed by a multitude of thoughts provoked by Jesus' attitude, approached him and asked for an explanation: "Son, why have you treated us so? Behold, your father and I have been looking for you anxiously." Her words are laden with pain and surprise, as if she were deeply disappointed. Perhaps she had expected, like any other mother in her place, that Jesus would throw himself into her arms, crying, embracing her with great emotion; but instead of this most normal, logical, and natural reaction, to all appearances Jesus had not even missed them.

It almost seems as if Mary's reaction is that of a mother scolding her son because he has got into mischief or has misbehaved; but the tone, the way in which she addresses Jesus, gives the impression that there is something she cannot completely understand, that she is not fully convinced that her Son has done something wrong in acting as he did, that there must be something that she cannot quite grasp; she cannot believe that her Son has acted in such a way as this. It seems as if the thing that disturbs her most, the thing that is behind her reproach is not what Jesus did but that now, when they are reunited, he does not show any of that same anguish, anxiety, and suffering that she has endured. Perhaps for the first time their feelings are not in agreement. Thus, there is more surprise than anything else in the painful tone of her words; her astonishment may be due to the fact that here she finds a different Jesus, completely unknown to her, completely changed.

Mary's maternal instinct on this point was not mistaken. The answer Jesus gave was, in fact, the answer of a person unknown to her: "How is it that you sought me? Did you not know that I must be in my Father's house?" She could not recognize the twelve-year-old boy whom she had seen grow up; she could hardly believe that this was the same child she had lost a few days before. These were profound and powerful words, spoken not by an ordinary child of twelve but by someone with authority. These were not the words of a child to his mother, but the words of one person who knows his duty to another who should know hers.

It is impossible to understand this passage of the Gospel unless we take into consideration a number of small but important circumstances that St. Luke fails to express and that we must fill in for ourselves. Consider, for example, the expression on their faces, their glances, the tone of their voices, the meaning of the words and phrases in the language in which they were originally spoken. But, however much we consider these things, it does not seem probable that we will find an explanation that will suit the taste of our own mentality. St. Luke ends his narration by saying: "And they did not understand the saying which he spoke to them." Everything here is full of great mystery. From Jesus' words we can deduce a certain surprise at the attitude of Mary and Joseph: "How is it that you sought me?" Then, as if reminding them of something they should know very well, he asks: "Did you not know that I must be in my Father's house? "

When we read the passage in St. Luke it seems as if the

Virgin reproaches Jesus and then Jesus reproaches Mary and Joseph. The first seems natural to us. After all, Mary was his mother, and he was only twelve years old. The second, however, seems strange, improper, and almost disrespectful. Our Lady must have been horrified. Nevertheless, it is inconceivable that Jesus would wish to hurt Mary and Joseph; it is unthinkable that his words could be disrespectful. They may seem hard to our mentality when translated into our own language, but obviously they were not so. They were simply objective, and an exact expression of what was going on in Jesus' mind at that moment.

Let us try to penetrate a little further into the significance of this event, without forgetting that it is and always will be a deep mystery. Evidently, the words of Jesus to his mother created a strange situation. It seems a little farfetched to think that Jesus had intended when he was going up to Jerusalem to stay behind in the Temple. If he decided to remain just when he should have been leaving with Mary and Joseph for home, he obviously did so in obedience to the will of his Father. Up to that moment, in view of our Lord's age, the Blessed Virgin had to act in the same way as any ordinary mother acts with a young child. Although he was God, Jesus obeyed; and she, although a creature and servant of the Lord, had commanded and guided her Son. Both had always had a singular, unique ability to perceive the will of God, both in perfect harmony, both always in perfect union with the Father's will. But the Son was greater than the Mother and was more united with God—the Son *is* God— and consequently he knew more immediately and more profoundly what God wished at any given moment. Besides, although in his humility he willed to become a child and live with the same helplessness and limitations as other children, this was so only as regards his human nature; as regards his mission as Messiah he was bound solely by the will of the Father. Jesus' messianic character did not manifest itself in his childhood; as a child he passed unnoticed among the other children like any other child. When the Virgin Mary asked him for an explanation, saddened by what he had done, she was fulfilling her duty; this was what she was obliged to do. Perhaps she thought that Jesus had actually been lost and had not left them willingly. To us it seems that the least Jesus could have done was to say that he was staying behind: he could, we think, have asked for permission. They could scarcely have refused it, knowing what they knew. They would have delayed their trip; they would have done anything that could possibly be done to enable Jesus to do as he wished. But that is not the way the Father wanted it. Jesus gave no explanation before leaving them, just as our Lady had given no explanation to Joseph even when the effects of the Incarnation began to manifest themselves in her. Christ's mission was to fulfill the wishes of his Father, and he was doing precisely that. This time, however, Mary did not understand so quickly and so profoundly the implications of what Jesus was doing. When Jesus asked: "How is it that you sought me?" he seemed a little surprised; and the next sentence explains his surprise. Knowing what they knew, how could they imagine that he could not find them if he were lost; how could they think that he would want to make them suffer? When they realized that he was not with them, they should have supposed that he had left them for some good reason; if he had left them it could only have been because of some higher command that required absolute obedience—the will of the Father.

Jesus did not ask for forgiveness. The words with which he answered his mother have about them a mysterious solemnity, and in them we see one thing clearly. Jesus confined Mary's right of intervention within limits she could not exceed. His mother's authority ended precisely in those things where he began to be independent of her, those things that pertained exclusively to the Father, the things concerning his mission.

Before that others had recognized the sovereign character of the King of Israel: the Magi, the shepherds, Simeon. But this is the first time that Jesus himself acts as the Messiah, and from this first act, he demands an absolute independence in his mission, without allowing even the slightest interference, not even on the part of his Mother.

The fact that our Lady did not understand her Son's

answer is in no way disedifying, nor does it in any way mar the brilliance of her perfection; on the contrary, for poor sinners like us, so full of misery and imperfections, it is most consoling—first, because it brings us very close to her, and second, because it shows us that our frequent incomprehension of the supernatural does not necessarily imply separation from God. In this case the Blessed Virgin did not understand. It is difficult to express all the implications to which St. Luke's observations give rise, but they are such as to emphasize the matchless perfection of Mary.

When she heard Jesus' answer, she must have felt very far from him; she must have keenly felt the deep sensation of bewilderment and separation that constantly reminded her of the immeasurable distance between the infinite and the finite.

The two planes of existence

We must never forget that there exist two distinct worlds, but not really separated from one another; two planes of existence, each having its own limits, its own laws and characteristics. There is a human plane in man's existence, a physical world that surrounds him and in which he moves. But there is a supernatural world to which he also belongs and which he cannot ignore, a superior level of existence to which man is so closely linked that he cannot escape from it. From what has been said it must be sufficiently clear that God's plan and human destiny exist absolutely and independently of, and superior to, merely biological factors or an individual's personal intervention. Man's acts, the acts of his intelligence and will, even the exercise of his freedom, are all confined within certain limits that he cannot licitly surpass without showing ignorance or rebelliousness, without showing his complete impotence in regard to the superior world.

Within the plane of human existence there exists a whole variety of relationships that are influenced by many diverse factors and whose intensity depends upon the force by which they are created. In the course of our lives we meet many people and develop many relationships. We have relationships with our neighbors, our business acquaintances, the people who belong to our political party, our pupils or our teachers; we have biological relationships with our parents or children; we have relationships with our friends, the people we like, those we love. To grade the different kinds of relationships between people in hierarchical order would present many difficult problems. But obviously there are some relationships that are natural, part of the nature of things, and therefore necessary, such as the relationship between father and son; there are other relationships that are not necessary, such as membership of a political party or a golf club. It would seem that the "necessary" relationships, those created by nature itself, must be more intense, and therefore must come in a hierarchy of values before those which are "not necessary," or artificial. Nevertheless, it is quite common to find the tie between members of the same political group, for instance, stronger and more intense than the tie between members of the same family, as if a voluntary association were more important than an association based on nature, at least as regards intensity. Again those relationships which stem from the affections—mutual attraction, friendship or love—prove to be much stronger unifying factors than those which are purely biological or intellectual. Thus, if we were to classify the various relationships according to strength of the bond between individuals, it seems that the ties based on the affections would be first, those stemming from the intellect would be second, and those based solely on biological factors would be last. In simpler language we can say that the strongest link is that of the heart, then the head, and lastly the blood.

This, of course, will surprise most people, especially since the relationship between parents and children, the blood link, is so strong that it cannot be broken; no one can cease to be the son of his parents or the parent of his children. But union does not depend on the link but on the quality of link. Two men handcuffed together and put in the same cell may be worlds apart in spite of their physical nearness; on the other hand, two friends, even though separated by continents, can still be joined in a strong, profound friendship. It is not any mere physical force that guarantees and cements a relationship. Nor is it any biological link. The love of parents for their children—the strongest of all—is not simply a biological or instinctive love, although instinct plays an important part, especially in the mother; no, it is something that comes from the heart, because the children are the fruit of the love between the parents, a palpable expression of the love between husband and wife; the parents' love is prolonged in the children in whom they continue to love each other. When the parents are united not by any deep heartfelt love but merely the animal instinct of sex, then they do not love the children. This is why children who are born out of wedlock may be condemned by their own parents to some orphanage or abandoned to some mercenary hands or to the shame of not being recognized. The fact that they are of the same blood means absolutely nothing. This point is well illustrated in a recent novel, set in China, in which a farmer's wife, who has been married for only three months, is violated by the Japanese, who first kill her husband; a few days after her son is born she kills him because he may be Japanese.

It is part of God's plan that the bond of love should be the first. Love between a man and woman is placed above even the natural relationship between parents and children, since for a woman shall a man "leave his father and mother and be joined to his wife; and the two shall become one" (Mt 19: 5). The bond of union between the members of any community, of whatever nature, is undoubtedly not so much the bond of blood or of intelligence but simply love; a love that gives way, or should give way, only to duty. This is not a contradiction, for duty is but the manifestation of a higher kind of love, although frequently it is less palpable.

The more we study the different relationships between people, the more we become convinced that love, that force which stems from our affections, ultimately triumphs over all others, even over the "necessary" factors. Love is stronger than death. Love alone lasts beyond the grave, because everything else that influences the relationships between men is destroyed by death, if it lasts even that long.

Now, human love, the strongest and noblest in the world, human love—not instinct or mere physical attraction, which is merely the animal side—while it springs from the most noble and most pure element in man, is nevertheless but a pale reflection of God. God, as St. John says, *is* Love (1 Jn 4: 8). If the essence of God is love, and if we are made in the image and likeness of God, our love will be genuine, true, only when it is a reflection of God, that is, when it leads us to him. Otherwise it is a diversion and a deformity. When, either in reality or in literature (especially novels), we hear of love that justifies the non-fulfillment of duty then it is a lie—that is not love: it is the corruption and the falsification of love. The link that, in the final analysis, joins us strongly and irrevocably to God is love. We exist precisely because God loved us from all eternity, before the beginning of time; to that love we owe the fact that we were chosen to exist out of all the possible creatures who could have taken our place. When we are joined to other human beings by love, which comes from our will, we do not leave the plane of nature; but when this love leads us to its source, then we transcend the limits of nature and penetrate into the supernatural world.

In this supernatural world God is the beginning and the end: he is everything. Because he is love, in his world—the world of grace—love is everything. But while we live on this earth there is no direct connection between one soul and another on the supernatural plane. What joins two souls—that is to say, two persons, since we are in this world—is the love of God; two people are united in God, by God, through God, and with God. Since this love of God is above nature, it is not subject to nature's laws. Mere human love, however noble, pure, elevated it may be, because it is human, is subject to all the laws of nature; it is a link that is broken by death. The only love that can endure forever is the love that is above death and over which death has no power.

Thus, within the range of human relationships, but on a higher level than the others, there exists another type of bond: supernatural, invisible, but more solid and intimate, that we cannot feel—except by a miracle—but that is more real; unobservable except by the grace of faith, but very much alive. It is a relationship founded on grace, which has its origin in the will illuminated and aided by God, and is the only one that endures forever. This invisible network, which comes from the love of God, binds together the great supernatural family of God's children "who were born, not of blood nor of the will of the flesh nor of the will of man, but of God" (Jn 1:13) by means of grace. This union brought about by supernatural love is firmer and more intense than any human relationship, in spite of the fact that it has an outward appearance. From this it follows that two Christians who are in the state of grace but have never even seen each other are more united than a father and son if one of them is in sin; and the union will grow stronger and closer in proportion to the intensity of the love of God in their souls. Furthermore, at death all the natural links between men, all differences of race, color, and country, disappear; all relationships based on blood, on the will of the flesh or the will of man, vanish: "For when they shall rise from the dead, they neither marry nor are given in marriage, but are like angels in heaven" (Mk 12:25).

There is a passage of the Gospel that throws some light on this question. Our Lord was in the house of Peter at Capharnaum, teaching the people: "While he was still speaking to the people, behold, his mother and his brethren stood outside, asking to speak to him. But he replied to the man who told him, 'Who is my mother, and who are my brethren?' And stretching forth his hand toward his disciples, he said, 'Here are my mother and my brethren! For whoever does the will of my Father in heaven is my brother, and sister, and mother' " (Mt 12:46–50).

The meaning of these lines is clear. Obviously Jesus is not trying to humiliate his Mother, for no one better than he knew the perfection with which she always—much more than the disciples—did the will of his Father. The man who was speaking to Jesus, however, did not see beneath the surface of what Jesus said; he knew nothing of the interior world; he knew only of the world of flesh and blood. This man could understand the words "brother" and "mother" only in their biological sense; and our Lord, in answering, revealed to him the vast horizons of supernatural relations with their own laws. Union with Jesus Christ, in whom we are saved, is realized by fulfilling the will of the Father; Jesus is the First Born among the brethren; Christ is our brother. The only real family, the family that endures beyond death and is indestructible because it is supernatural and founded on grace, is the family composed of the children of God, the brothers of Christ, united with him in the Father who is in Heaven. These words of Jesus are very illuminating; they lift a corner of that veil which conceals the mysteries that lie beyond death. Jesus makes many things clear to us. He shows that the strongest link between him and his Mother was in their union with God, a link far more important than the fact that they had the same blood in their veins. Among other things, these words of Christ explain why he would not allow this link to be weakened by the ties of the flesh even at the cost of causing suffering in his parents when he was in the Temple.

The fourth commandment

On reading this episode of Jesus in the Temple, and especially the short dialogue at the end, one is immediately and unconsciously inclined to take the side of Mary; but this feeling is banished by the thought that Jesus is God. At first the scene appears to be merely a problem between mother and son; a Mother who has suffered and wept for many days, and a Son who is scarcely twelve years old and has willingly left his parents without saying a word about where he was going or where they could find him. It seems to be a case of insubordination, a trivial escapade to be sure, but one that we cannot ignore. In a case like this, the mother fulfills her duty by reprimanding the child, and the child should not answer back because he has no excuse.

In this passage of the Gospel, however, we are not dealing with an ordinary case of a child's disobedience, because the mother is the *gratia plena*, full of grace, the most perfect and most holy of creatures, and the Son is Jesus, more perfect than the mother because he is God.

Jesus did not remain silent; he could not; he was obeying his Father, who is above all creatures. Nevertheless, when Jesus returned to Nazareth, he was "obedient to them" (Lk 2:51). This phrase summarizes the conduct of Jesus toward Mary and Joseph for the following eighteen years. He was subject to them, but this did not make him cease to be supernaturally free. Subjection—obedience—is not, then, incompatible with freedom but, instead, represents freedom coupled with order.

We must have both subjection and freedom in regard to our parents. Even though one person is the object of both attitudes, still there is no incompatibility between them. When Jesus obeyed Mary and Joseph—as he did for thirty years—he was still perfectly free. There was a thin but very clear line that marked off another sphere in which Jesus, as well as being free, was independent; that is, in that sphere which borders on the human plane of existence but is very much superior to it. In that sphere he depended only on the Father and was accountable only to him. The dependence of children on their parents extends only to the divinely established limits of the parents' jurisdiction; it extends no further. Thus, a father cannot order his son to tell him matters of conscience, matters that the son will easily reveal in sacramental confession. Each one's interior life, what may be called the realm of conscience, is nothing else than the register, so to speak, of the relationship between the soul and God, and between God and the soul.

It is true that parents have a special grace of state to help and enlighten them in the education of their children, in the same way that a priest has special graces to aid him in his priestly tasks. It would be absurd, however, to expect the grace of state given a priest to be helpful in solving strictly financial or professional questions, that is to say, when there are no moral implications; the grace of state that the priest receives is specifically to help him in his ministerial functions and does not help him in determining how money should be invested or what kind of technical books a person should read in his spare time. There is no obligation on anyone to follow the advice of a priest in anything outside his priestly function, for his opinion in these other fields is merely a personal one and his competence depends on his knowledge of the subject in question.

It is much the same with parents. To interfere in matters that are not completely and exclusively within their juris-diction—as, for example, the spiritual life of their children —can have disastrous effects. Thus, forcing children to fre-quent the sacraments can lead to the committing of sacri-lege; on the contrary, to forbid the frequenting of the sacraments can lead the children into sin for lack of interior nourishment and strength. To force a child to go to a certain confessor or to forbid him to go to some other may cause serious harm; no one can exceed the limits set by the Church on these matters. Parents have the duty of safeguarding, en-couraging and helping their children in spiritual matters, especially when they are very young, but without interfering with the child's privacy of conscience. Children may freely confide in their parents, but the parents should not forget that in regard to spiritual matters a priest is the person who has grace of state, and in these matters the children must be independent: they depend not on their parents but on God, who created their souls without anyone's help.

In everything else the children must be subject to their parents; they must obey them, but freely and not as slaves; a child can obey freely only if he loves those on whom he depends and from whom he takes orders.

This subjection of children to parents is not always the same. It extends from the absolute dependence of the newly-born infant who can do nothing for himself to the complete independence of the married man with a family. But this does not in any way diminish the obligatory force of the Fourth Commandment, for it does not order us simply to "obey" our parents but something else, which includes obe-dience and much more; that is, what Jesus said, among other things, to the man who desired to do good to the best of his ability: "Honor your father and mother" (Lk 18: 20).

We must notice here a curious relationship between the obligations that a child owes to his parents and those that he owes to his Father, God. The parents are like representatives of God in relation to their children; their authority comes from their cooperation with God in his plan of procreation. It is not enough, however, to obey God like automatons; we must love him, and only then will we give him what we owe him: glory. Our mission is to give glory to God. In the same way it is not enough to obey our parents; we must love them, because only then can we honor them. It may seem that the distinction between honoring and obeying is too subtle; this, however, is not the case. If the Fourth Commandment required merely obedience to parents, then when children grew up or got married they would be exempt from this obedience, and the commandment would lose all its strength; it would be only a temporary commandment valid up to a certain age or state—which is, of course, absurd. On the other hand, although there comes a time in life when we must no longer obey our parents, we must always honor them.

What the Fourth Commandment requires is that we love and respect our parents, make them happy, obey them, and act in such a way as to make them proud of us, their children, and by our actions to reflect honor on them. It is not enough merely to obey and avoid friction. There are many children who do not even argue or quarrel with their parents but ignore them completely. The Fourth Commandment is not a negative precept; in order to keep it fully it is not enough merely to avoid giving trouble. Anything that would shame our parents in any way is opposed to the spirit and letter of the Fourth Commandment. It is really painful to see the lamentable ignorance that children frequently have of their duties toward their parents, and the narrow limits within which they confine them. It is not common, for example, to find a student confessing that he broke the Fourth Commandment by being lazy or by failing an examination, and yet such laxity is precisely what reflects shame on the parents. Neither is it common to accuse ourselves of breaking the Fourth Commandment by omission, when actually this is the most common way it is broken.

In the Scripture there is little insistence on the obligation of parents to love their children because, after all, this is something they need hardly be reminded of. On the other hand, children are frequently reminded of their obligations to their parents. Parents live for their children, hoping in them, worrying about them, making a thousand plans for their future, dreaming; it is a law of nature strongly ingrained in their being, and they do not need to be reminded about it. Children, on the other hand, do not live for their parents. Life for them always flows forward, never backward. When parents look at their children, they look in the direction in which life flows. The children also have a tendency to look ahead to the future stretched out before them; they plan their own lives for the long years they see before them. And because they tend to think only of themselves and forget their parents according as they grow up, Scripture frequently reminds them of their duty to honor those people who gave them birth. "They must be helped to understand the simple, natural, and often unappreciated beauty of their parents' lives. Children should come to realize, little by little, the sacrifices their parents have made for them, the often heroic self-denial that has gone into raising the family. They should also learn not to overdramatize, not to think themselves misunderstood; nor to forget that they will always be in debt to their parents. And as they will never be able to repay what they owe, their response should be to treat their parents with veneration and grateful, filial love." [1]

And he "was subject to them." In this subjection there is something more than mere obedience. A child obeys if he does what he is commanded, but parents do not spend their lives giving orders. There is a gradual scale of obedience, which extends from the forced and mechanical obedience of a slave to the free and sensitive obedience born of love. It is because of his love for Mary and Joseph that Jesus was subject to them when he was no longer a child but a man. Obedience, the submission of children to their parents, must be a result of their love. Love makes us seek our happiness in the happiness of those we love, and thus it is the obligation of children to honor and not simply obey their parents.

[1] J. Escrivá de Balaguer, *Conversations*, no. 101.

When there is love there is tenderness, and when there is tenderness orders and commands are unnecessary; a slight hint suffices, and many times even that is not needed because the mere desires of those we love are guessed and satisfied. "Following her example of obedience to God, we can learn to serve delicately without being slavish. In Mary we don't find the slightest trace of the attitude of the foolish virgins, who obey, but thoughtlessly. Our Lady listens attentively to what God wants, ponders what she doesn't fully understand, and asks about what she doesn't know. Then she gives herself completely to doing the divine will: 'Behold, I am the handmaid of the Lord; let it be to me according to your word' (Lk 1: 38). Isn't that marvelous? The Blessed Virgin, our teacher in all we do, shows us here that obedience to God is not servile, does not bypass our conscience. We should be inwardly moved to discover the 'freedom of the children of God' (Rom 8: 21)." [2]

With a little reflection, and considering what we said before, we can easily conclude that the link that should join children to their parents is love—a human love, of course, since we are humans. This love for our parents is the result of our parents' love for us, their kindness, their sacrifices, the suffering we have caused them; it is strengthened by the memory of a thousand little everyday things, the happy hours of our childhood, when our parents were everything to us. We owe our parents a debt that can be paid only with love; countless are the things that they have given to us, including our being itself. For us they have become children again; they have loved us deeply with the purest and deepest love in this world, and in us they have come closer to one another. If we love a person, we want to do things for him, and therefore children should fight against their own selfishness, which unfortunately too often makes them prefer to satisfy their own desires than to give their parents little pleasures or even big pleasures. Children should make the effort to find their own happiness in the happiness they see in their parents. How often do they hurt their parents by being too

[2] J. Escrivá de Balaguer, *Christ Is Passing By*, no. 173.

lazy to write or to write on time! How often do they cause worry or unhappiness in their parents by being too comfort-loving or too inconsiderate—too selfish, in other words—to do things or not to do things which take very little effort! This applies to children of all ages; but older children have a graver obligation, for, since their intelligence is more developed and the precept of obedience more relaxed, they should be more particular about their love and tenderness and other details of affection.

However, it is not a question of purely human love. The lasting ties with our parents must always be related to the love of God. Our love for our parents must be not only human but also supernatural. Moreover, if we truly love our parents, this love will of necessity be supernatural, because it is the only love that survives intact after death. Only when our love for our parents has this supernatural basis can we say that it is real, because only then is it grounded on the solid and stable foundation of the will and not in the inconstant and hazy foundation of the sentiments. This love, then, like all real love, desires to perpetuate itself for ever beyond the limits of time, and it is not satisfied by human standards but looks only to eternity. It seeks stability, finality, and permanence; it does not allow human love to destroy supernatural love nor does it allow the tie that unites us to our parents to be loosened by trivialities. This love, then, which nothing can destroy, is not instinctive but "willed," voluntary, and conscious and thereby gains in freshness and spontaneity; it is supernatural and human at the same time, taking into consideration the hierarchy of duties in their proper order and fulfilling them all without neglecting any.

This explains why, in certain cases, we are obliged by the Fourth Commandment to go against our parents' wishes in order to give them the honor which is their due and which God prescribes. Let us take the case of parents who are opposed to a child giving himself completely to God at the expense, perhaps, of a successful future. It is evident that if the child truly loves his parents, he will not relinquish his vocation in order to obey them; if he did he could be laying on their consciences the tremendous responsibility of the loss of his vocation; instead of honoring them, he could thus do them an injury, perhaps an eternal injury. Physical separation matters little and, besides, it is inevitable: founding a new family always implies disrupting another, the new family beginning the vital cycle all over again. What is really terrible is the separation of two people who live together and—as in the example above—there is no separation greater than two people who live far from God.

Jesus, the same Jesus who reprimanded the Pharisees for the subtle ways they avoided living according to the Fourth Commandment, who reminds us that we should honor our father and mother, then says: "He who loves father or mother more than me is not worthy of me; and he who loves son or daughter more than me is not worthy of me" (Mt 10: 37). The same sweet and obedient Jesus who filled so many hours in the life of the Virgin with the joy and peace of his luminous presence, then left her for three days and later left her for good when he was thirty years old—when she was left alone, when she needed him most! But Mary would not have been so honored as she is today if our Lord had not done precisely that.

On the other hand, the demands of God, the service of the Father, are too serious a matter to allow them to hide our own selfishness or to use them as a pretext to avoid obligations that are imposed on us by God. This would be to fall into the very sin of the Pharisees condemned by our Lord (Mk 7: 2ff.).

The duty of honoring our parents lasts for ever because, even though heaven and earth pass away, God's word will not pass away (Mk 13: 31). There is no excuse for anyone who can give his parents pleasure and does not; nor for anyone who humiliates his parents instead of acting in such a way as to make them proud of him; nor for anyone who gives them shame and sadness when with a little care and consideration he could fill them with happiness. It is astounding to see the blindness of many children in regard to their duties under the Fourth Commandment when it is so easy—and even if it were difficult—to make parents happy.

Marriage, a vocation

It has been mentioned that marriage is a vocation (cf. *The Way*, no. 27), and it would be good to examine that statement further. One must not think of marriage as a "residuary" vocation, that is to say, left to those who have no other better or more elevated vocation open to them. There exists a divine order for the procreation of the species through the union of man and woman; to this union everyone is called in a general way; but some special individuals whom God needs free of ties are exempt (cf. *The Way*, no. 28). "For a Christian, marriage is not just a social institution, much less a mere remedy for human weakness. It is a real supernatural calling."[3] The greater or lesser intensity of the call to marriage depends both on the extent of the individual's dependence on God and on the extent to which God wants him for his own service.

Marriage has been considered as a "residuary" vocation for so long, possibly due to a constant insistence among the faithful on the greater excellence of the state of virginity. It is not infrequent for a truth to give rise to an erroneous way of thinking, collectively, in the public mind. The "public," the collective mentality of large groups, usually grasps only the most general principles, without any subtle explanation or precision; only in the most rudimentary and simple forms do concepts survive in the public mind.

Undoubtedly, in the absolute order, the exclusive dedication of oneself to God and the Church, complete self-surrender to the service of God, is something superior, more perfect, and—on the human level—more elegant than marriage, which implies a withholding of part of oneself even if it is withheld in order to give it, not without a certain self-interest, to another person. Marriage has a number of compensations in the human order that are sacrificed by those who dedicate themselves completely to God. Only narrow-minded and very unintelligent people can be shocked by the statement that "Marriage is for the rank and file, not for the

---

[3] *Christ Is Passing By*, no. 23.

officers of Christ's army."[4] The rank and file are absolutely necessary in any army, but without leaders it would be all but impossible to direct their action in a war fought along a wide front. This job of direction requires special and exclusive dedication in the army of Christ. Even though it was possible at the time of St. Paul for a man who was married—but only once—to become a bishop, the Church has little by little imposed celibacy on her priests because she needs them without ties and without duties other than those pertaining to the service of the Church. Everyone to whom God has entrusted the care of souls should be free of worries of an inferior kind, that is, worries of a purely natural order. In the encyclical *Sacra Virginitas* Pope Pius XII forestalled certain possible errors that might originate in the collective mind from today's excessive insistence on the excellence of matrimony.

But if we descend from the general and absolute order to the level of the individual, to the concrete life of each person, then the best and worst, the higher and lower in the absolute order, cease to be important; for then the best thing for every man is what God has planned for him; the best thing for the individual is the way that God has chosen for him independently of whether, in a scale of values considered in themselves, it be more humble than other ways or the most humble of all. As St. Paul says: "Each has his own special gift from God, one of one kind and one of another" (1 Cor 7: 7). "Love, which leads to marriage and family, can also be a marvelous divine way, a vocation, a path for a complete dedication to our God. Do things perfectly, I have reminded you. Put love into the little duties of each day; discover that *divine something* contained in these details. All this teaching has a special place in that area of life where human love has its setting."[5] "What is really important is that each person should follow his own vocation. For each individual, the most perfect thing is, always and only, to do God's will."[6]

---

[4] J. Escrivá de Balaguer, *The Way*, no. 28.
[5] *Conversations*, no. 121.
[6] *Conversations*, no. 92.

Matrimony as a vocation thus acquires a grandeur much greater than it usually has in the consciences of many married people. When St. Paul called marriage the "great sacrament," it was not just an idle compliment: St. Paul was inspired by God, so it is God himself who speaks of marriage in this way.

A sacrament is a holy thing, something sacred. It is a means established by God for our sanctification, as are holy orders and all the other sacraments. Matrimony then, being a sacrament, is something that sanctifies, something that makes saints. It is not merely a licit means of satisfying the demands of instinct; on the contrary, these demands derive their *raison d'être* from matrimony because it is the end to which the sexes are directed. But we know that the end of every human creature from the moment he is created is to give glory to God by fulfilling the divine will, by carrying out his own particular mission in life. The end of marriage, in the final analysis, is the glory of God through personal sanctification, making use of the precise means that God offers those to whom he gives this particular vocation, since he instituted matrimony expressly for this purpose.

It is true that no one ever thought that marriage must prevent sanctity—since this would be tantamount to denying the sanctifying power of a sacrament. However, in actual practice this way of life has commonly been regarded rather curiously by people, almost as if it were the "worse part" in contrast to the "better part" chosen by the religious, a renouncement of holiness, as if holiness were a patrimony reserved to those souls that have abandoned the "world" and its temporal affairs.

On this matter, as on so many others, St. Josemaría Escrivá has opened up broad prospects, not only by stressing the fact that marriage has the character of a vocation, a calling by God ("Do you laugh because I tell you that you have a 'vocation to marriage'? Well, you have just that—a vocation." [7]) but also by gathering the consequences of this real fact. Writes he: "While teaching a dogmatic fact, that

[7] *The Way*, no. 27.

virginity—or perfect chastity—is superior to matrimony, I have told married couples that they too can be contemplative souls in their state of life, precisely in the fulfilment of their familial obligation."[8]

The *ascende superius* (Lk 14: 10) is not, therefore, an exclusive feature of a particular condition of life. It is an invitation filled with possibilities addressed to all, including those who are married; an invitation that dislodges no one from, but rather leaves each one in, the same place and position he occupies in the world. St. Josemaría Escrivá has with good reason concluded that "*the divine paths of the earth* have been thrown open to all souls."

Again, to feel at present the words of St. Paul to the Corinthians: "But as the Lord hath distributed to every one, as God hath called every one; so let him walk. . . . Let every man abide in the same calling in which he was called. . . . Let every man, wherein he was called, therein abide with God. . . . Art thou bound to a wife? Seek not to be loosed" (1 Cor 7: 20, 24, 27), because it is there, in the state in which God has placed us, that we will find perfection. We will either find it there or, probably, nowhere.

Matrimony is the origin of the Christian family, and every Christian family is like a cell of that living organism we call the Church. In their families young Christians learn to know God, to pray to him, to look on him as their Father, to pray to the Blessed Virgin. From Christian families come the priests, other Christs, that spread good doctrine and administer the sacraments. The family is necessary for the perpetuation of the Church, to fill the ranks of the faithful. And because without marriage there would be no families, it is obvious that God wants this way, which is therefore for many people, those who are called to this vocation, as important as, for example, their own way is for the religious. It is imperative that married people should keep this in mind; they must not think that marriage has meant losing the opportunity of doing something great with their lives; they must not consider financial worries, children, the fight for

[8] Letter, March 19, 1954.

life, the noble, clean, and natural happiness that they enjoy or the little frictions that occur in their family life together, as so many obstacles that prevent them from reaching perfection, sanctity, and union with God. This is a grave error, because these are precisely the things in which they will find God. It is all these ordinary things which they must sanctify with God's grace; these things are the instrument God uses to make them perfect, provided that they desire perfection and cooperate with God, doing everything that he expects of them. "Any one who thinks that love ends when the worries and difficulties that life brings with it begin, has a poor idea of marriage, which is a sacrament and an ideal and a vocation. It is precisely then that love grows strong. Torrents of worries and difficulties are incapable of drowning true love because people who sacrifice themselves generously together are brought closer by their sacrifice. As Scripture says, *aquae multae*—a host of difficulties, physical and moral—*non potuerunt extinguere caritatem*—cannot extinguish love (Song 8: 7)." [9]

This notion of marriage as a vocation, as a way of acquiring sanctity, holds enormous potentials. Here, perhaps more than in any other case, it is possible to realize the extent to which every rational being should be an intelligent instrument in the hands of God and to which everything he does should be in collaboration with God. Not that a married man is a better instrument or can collaborate with God better than anyone else, but in married life the facts are more tangible, and it is easier to see with concrete clarity the actual collaboration of the creature with God.

The principal end of marriage is procreation. God made and ordered nature in such a way that he wished the union of man and woman in order to produce children. But this is not the work merely of a man and a woman. Their union, of course, is indispensable and is of such force that for a woman a man shall "leave his father and mother and be joined to his wife, and the two shall become one" (Mt 19: 5). It does not, however, involve merely two, but three. The man and the

[9] *Conversations*, no. 91.

woman cooperate with each other, but also with God. They use the natural powers, which God gave them, to form the body of the child, and God infuses a soul into that body. Between the three of them they bring new lives into the world.

God always does his part; he always infuses a soul into the body, and this is true also in the case where the new being is the result of sin. Besides, there is no doubt that having children is a task laden with worries, as well as a grave and serious responsibility; that is why God endows the act of procreation with a great amount of pleasure and places in men and women a strong sexual instinct. From this we can see how monstrous a crime it is to commit a fraud in marriage, for fundamentally it involves scorn and deceit thrown in the face of God. The misuse of marriage, taking only the physical pleasure and avoiding conception, directly attacks the sanctity of the sacrament; and to reduce the act of procreation to a sterile pleasure is a kind of sacrilege which prostitutes the union of the partners and makes them conspirators against God. "Everything becomes clouded, because husband and wife begin to look at each other as accomplices, and the dissensions that are produced, if this state is allowed to continue, are almost always impossible to heal. . . . When the divine gift of sex is perverted, their intimacy is destroyed, and they can no longer look openly at each other." [10] This is a sin which is always paid for, even in this life, because it is an act of extreme selfishness and separates, just as love unites. Such sins spring from a completely human view of marriage, a view not in the least supernatural; for when matrimony is considered merely as a means of legitimatizing sexual relationships that would otherwise be unlawful, it is difficult—indeed impossible—to think of it as a means of sanctification.

The correct view of marriage is very different. God has given us considerable proofs of his love, not the least of which is the fact that he has honored us by associating us with himself in the act of procreation. Only God is the Cre-

[10] *Christ Is Passing By*, no. 25.

ator. Man and woman simply help him, and they should always respect the conditions that he has imposed. Taking all these things into consideration, we can now see marriage in all its impressive dignity. Only when those who decide to unite together for life realize fully and deeply the great dignity of marriage will they adequately appreciate the sacrament; only then will they consider matrimony not merely as something to legitimatize their union, but to *sanctify* it; only then will they have a complete understanding of what marriage is. Besides being familiar with the encyclical *Casti Connubii*, married couples should also read *Marriage, A Great Sacrament*, by J. Leclercq, and the excellent chapter on "Marriage and Sanctity" in the second volume of *This Tremendous Lover*, by Eugene Boylan.

Collaboration in marriage, however, is not limited merely to what concerns procreation. The new being that comes into the world needs his parents for many years; he is absolutely dependent on them, unable in any way to help himself, entirely abandoned to the care of those who gave him life. This does not mean, however, that the parents are left entirely to their own devices, to do whatever suits them best. God still stands by. Parenthood does not mean ownership of a child. The rights of God over children are far superior to those of the parents or the community. After all, parents cannot even choose their children but God chooses everyone's parents.

It is an unfortunate fact that most couples when they get married are not adequately trained for the education of their future children. It is surprising to see the contrast between the years spent working for a university degree, for instance, that will enable one to teach, and the little time spent in preparing for the education of one's own children. It is very common for parents to forget that each child has a personality of his own, given to him by God, and forgetting this they try to make their children little copies of themselves. Since it is God who gave them, with their soul, an individuality of their own, special talents, a specific degree of intelligence, and who, all during their lives, gives them enormous variety of graces according to the circumstances in which he sees them, it is obvious that the God who has fixed their destiny should also direct and guide their lives. This is where the danger of parents exceeding the boundaries of their own jurisdiction is greatest. There is danger in the two extremes: either being too lax and not bothering about the child at all, letting him grow up like the weeds in the fields, or, going to the other extreme, being too strict, too concerned, trying to restrain the child's normal development until he becomes like a hothouse plant, harassed and overwhelmed by constant commands, with a false and deformed personality.

As we have already mentioned, there are certain spheres in which parents can at the most advise their children but cannot force them or even try to influence them too much. We can divide the educational function of parents into two parts: to help the children to develop their intelligence in such a way that when the time comes they will be able to see what God wants of them, and to strengthen their will so as to be independent and able to follow their own vocation in life. God relies on parents to help their children find out what they should do and encourage them to do it; to prepare their children to face life in such a way as to give glory to God without being seduced by the world; to help their children to be happy both here and in the next life, to serve God and save their souls. The parents' role is to do much more than merely provide their children with a secure and prosperous future. The formation of children requires a great deal of attention, constant care, and close observation; the parents must learn to understand each child and gain his confidence. It is not enough to have authority; they must be friends of their children and understand them, always being careful not to exceed their proper limits. It is not a question of governing the children by means of orders—a Christian home is not a barracks—but of forming them so that, like Jesus, they grow up "in wisdom and age and grace with God and men" (Lk 2:52). They should help their children to develop harmoniously the natural gifts that God has given them; they should be on their guard against any deformity or mistakes, helping children to understand the why and wherefore of things so that they will develop a sound judgment.

When parents try to do too much, they run the risk of interfering with the action of the Holy Spirit, with whom they should cooperate but not try to replace. The lack of supernatural outlook, the purely human, non-Christian judgment of parents who call themselves and are Christians, is seen especially when a child has a vocation to a life of perfection. In these cases there is not usually a sharp opposition, a straight refusal; however unchristian the parents are or however little common sense they have, it is very difficult to oppose God and stand in the way of someone's personal decision. What commonly does happen is that they advise the child to wait a little, to be sure, with the excuse of testing his vocation. It is a subtle deceit because, at least to all appearances, they wish only his own good, that he be sure of his vocation, that he should test it, in order to make everyone concerned happy. In the first place it is not the function of parents to test anyone's vocation: to test it is the same as to tempt, and how sad it is to see parents tempt their own children. And in the second place it allows the devil an ample margin of time so that he can leisurely get to work in making chaos out of the life of the person involved. The devil does not like to see anyone give himself to God, because in that way he loses many souls. Consider, on the contrary, how willingly they guide their children toward marriage, and this too is for life. The same is true, for example, when it is a question of choosing a profession or career. It cannot be denied that parents cannot and should not ignore these problems, but their function is only to advise—and to advise not with the prudence of the flesh, but the prudence of the spirit, not with human standards, but with supernatural outlook, never losing sight of their duty to collaborate with God, never directing their children solely according to their own interests. They should seek the happiness and welfare of their children, and it may be that their children will find happiness in a different way than they themselves found it. Legitimate but too human sentiments—for instance, desire for grandchildren, security in their old age, the success of their children in the world—may cloud and even obliterate parents' awareness of God's will; unconsciously they may even try to replace the will of God with their own desires, defending their will as if it were God's.

Because we are human and each of us has his own personality, friction or even violent disagreements can surprise nobody. There are times in life when questions of such importance arise that one must make gigantic efforts to avoid being overwhelmed by them, to maintain serenity and a supernatural outlook. There are moments, sometimes decisive moments, in which parents experience sorrow and anguish from situations brought about either by their children or by their children and themselves; an anxiety similar to our Lady's, the sensation of having lost a son or daughter because they have given themselves to God and no longer belong to their parents; a sense of complete separation, of no longer being able to count on them. They do not see that separation is impossible while there is supernatural love, which is the only love that lasts; nor do they realize that when God gives children a vocation, he gives another vocation to the parents. The children's vocation is to give themselves to God while the vocation of the parents is to give to God what they love most in the world. In these cases the children suffer too (just as Jesus suffered when he saw his mother's anguish)—and not only for themselves. But the will of the Father must always be fulfilled, even if it causes pain and suffering.

No one should interfere in things connected with the service of God: they are matters in which they have no concern. Since God made man in his own image and likeness, and since he respects his freedom even to the extent of preferring to be offended rather than undo his own work, parents should all the more fully respect the complete freedom of their children in those intimate things concerning the spiritual relations between the soul and God. Jesus' attitude to his mother and his answer when she asked him for an explanation of his conduct can teach us more than any treatise.

It is impossible, however, to fulfill completely and fully the primary end of marriage, the procreation and education of children, if its intrinsic characteristic, its essential property, is not maintained. That is the permanence, the unity and indivisibility of the union. This characteristic of marriage is not merely legal, but something that extends to the very heart of married life. Two people may be legally "united" and still remain worlds apart.

No romanticism could speak of human love in such beautiful terms as those in which the Holy Church blesses marital love. No one has as high a concept of marriage as the Church since she affirms that it is a means of sanctification, a divine vocation. A married couple may make their home a preview of heaven if they choose, because they will love each other only to the extent that they—consciously or unconsciously—love God, and they will give themselves to each other to the same extent that they give themselves to God. It is true that life is not all a bed of roses, but it is sad to see how many people abandon the hopes with which they entered marriage because they meet with a few hardships which, in fact, should bring them closer together. Nothing is useless in a Christian home: joys and sorrows, work and rest, poverty and abundance, success and failure, everything can be sanctified by the grace of Jesus Christ.

It is necessary, however, that the married couple should love one another always as if they were young lovers. They should not allow time or selfishness—seeking their own happiness rather than their partner's—or the hardships of life, or excessive plenty, to turn love into something boring, which drags on over the years with excruciating tedium. The secret of happiness in marriage lies in the ordinary little everyday things: details of dress, decoration of the house, the joy of coming home, the work and play in which the whole family cooperate together; these are the things that assure the continuance of love. And love is of extreme importance because without love there is no unity, and separation and division are the symptoms of death; "the secret of married happiness lies in everyday things, not in daydreams. It lies in finding the hidden joy of coming home in the evening; in affectionate relations with their children; in everyday work in which the whole family cooperates; in good humor in the face of difficulties that should be met with a sporting spirit." [11]

A great deal of a child's future depends on his home atmosphere. Many of those who give themselves to God and renounce the things of the world owe a great part of their vocation to the solicitude of their parents. How powerful are the prayers of a mother! And once more we repeat that it is the love of God which guarantees marital union and harmony and which gives depth even to the simplest of human attentions and elevates them into acts of charity, thus making the marriage partners not only one flesh but also one heart and one soul.

[11] *Conversations*, no. 91.

4

THE HIDDEN LIFE

But Mary kept all these words, pondering them in her
heart.

LUKE 2: 19

Interior life

These few words of St. Luke sum up in fact many years in
Mary's life. The period we may call the hidden life of Mary is
much longer than the period of silent obscurity in the life of
her Son. The only time we ever really see Mary is during
those few months when Jesus, as a helpless child, needs her
to help him. Later on in his life, the Virgin appears only
sporadically and secondarily and always in relation to some
act of her Son: the journey to Jerusalem, the episode in the
Temple, the wedding feast of Cana, another brief moment
when with some relatives and friends she went to look for
Jesus, and finally the crucifixion. The whole life of our Lady
was, in fact, a hidden life, because on those very rare occasions on which she came into the foreground she was noticed only by very few people. The Virgin Mary had no
public career.

In order to account for all these years of her life, that
long period of time, all the evangelist says is: "But Mary
kept all these words, pondering them in her heart." Certainly it is not very much. And yet it must be very important because a little later on, when the Holy Family had
returned to Nazareth after finding Jesus in the Temple, St.
Luke again insists on the very same idea, in almost the
same words: "And his mother kept all these things in her
heart" (Lk 2:51). He says the same thing twice without
adding anything. We, who would like to know many more
details about our Lady, feel a little disappointed because

our very understandable curiosity was not considered by the evangelist; we think it rather a pity that, since he knew so much about the Virgin, much of it probably from her own lips, he should not have been more explicit. On the other hand, the Gospels are the message of God, and God revealed to us exactly what we need to know. If we needed more details, he would have seen to it that they were recorded. There is no doubt that we know enough about the Blessed Virgin, even about her hidden life.

St. Luke's repeated remark is important not only for what it says, but also for what it does not say. Silence is often very revealing and can be thunderously eloquent. Could it not be that St. Luke did not say more simply because there was nothing more to say? It is true that the Gospels are, in a way, a summarized written account of the more extensive oral teachings of the apostles. There are many other items that continued to circulate only in the oral tradition, of which we can find accounts in the written documents of the Church, such as the liturgical texts and the letters of the apostles included in the canon of the New Testament. Nevertheless, we must not forget that the greatest and most important part of God's revelation has come down to us through sacred Scripture, the Gospels in particular. In order, then, to understand completely the lesson to be learned from the example of our Lady, we must first examine what St. Luke says, and then consider what he does not say.

So far, we know two things for certain: that the Blessed Virgin kept certain words in her mind and that she pondered them in her heart. That is to say, certain events, certain impressions affected her more deeply and engraved themselves on her memory more permanently than others. She does not merely remember them, however, but ponders on them. She did not live in the past; her soul was not a cemetery of dead and useless memories, a storehouse of times and events gone by. These things which she kept within herself had a value and a significance. The Virgin Mary was not a sentimental woman who would waste time nostalgically thinking over the past, as we sometimes do, and we find in that sweet sadness of remembrance an excuse for our laziness or weakness—the Virgin Mary was not like this. She did not let her imagination get the better of her; instead, she used her intelligence. To ponder things in the heart means to meditate on them, to think of them, to examine their meaning, to see how they are related to one another, to discover all their implications. To ponder things in the heart is to live an interior life, to exercise constantly, and perfect our interior powers to advance in wisdom. When we meditate on human things without that third dimension which is supernatural outlook, our meditation is nothing more than mere reflection; but when our supernatural outlook puts us in contact with God and the superior world, then we acquire an interior life in the true sense of the word.

Without this pondering on the things which are in the heart it is meaningless to speak of any real interior life. What gives value and importance in our personal life, to every act, every idea, every event, is that depth and understanding which show us its place in God's plan and our vocation. For spiritual advancement an interior life is essential. Confusion, superficiality, and frivolity cause in a man such interior poverty that it is easy to understand the terrible religious ignorance we find in such great multitudes of Christians. If our spiritual outlook on the world around us is superficial and inattentive, seeing only the external appearances of things and never perceiving their deeper meaning as part of God's overall plan in the universe, then creatures for us have no purpose other than their appearance; this attitude sooner or later weakens our faith, diminishes or extinguishes—as is so common among Christians—our supernatural outlook, and makes of our life a meaningless vacuum. There is then no sense in anything, not because it lacks meaning, but because the person has not even the minimum capacity to find it. When such superficiality becomes general—as it is today, for instance—we get that *standard* type of man and woman: who lack character, who are full of idle chatter, mass-produced, as it were, completely bored with life because they have not even the most elementary interior formation; they cannot carry on an intelligent conversation; after all, words are the expression of ideas, and a person who does not think can have very few ideas.

Reflection, pondering, leads to interior depth. For this, it is sufficient to belong to the human race. But in a Christian something more is required; that reflection must be tempered with something which only a Christian has: faith in Christ. This gives special quality to his mode of reflection, and makes him look on the universe in a different and deeper way than an atheist or a pagan. The greater and more alive a Christian's faith and the more intensely he has the spirit of Christ, the more meaningful the world around him becomes, and the more depth he discovers in people and events. The relationship between all things becomes more concrete and real. Finally, everything is changed and transformed, acquiring a special quality of transparency that enables him to see God; creatures take on clearer shapes, which let him see them as they really are: manifestations of the power of God, testimonies to his kindness and grandeur, silent but eloquent messengers of his will. Only he who ponders things in his heart with a true Christian spirit can discover the immense riches of the interior world, the world of grace, that hidden treasure which is within us all. To the people of this age and of all ages we can still apply St. John the Baptist's words addressed to those of his time: "Among you stands one whom you do not know" (Jn 1: 26).

It was by pondering things in her heart that Mary, as time went on, grew in understanding of the mystery, in sanctity and in unity with God. Contrary to the general impression we have, our Lady did not find everything done for her on her way to God; much effort was demanded of her, and she had to undergo many tests that no other human being—except her Son—could have endured. Much had been given to her, and much indeed was demanded of her. She was not an automaton but a woman, and she had to make a constant effort to be always ready for whatever was to come; she might be surprised, but never for a moment did she hesitate or doubt that it was all for the best, that it was God's plan for her; always accepting as most logical what human considerations would call madness, always keeping her serenity, every moment doing what God wanted her to do.

One cannot go deeply into the meaning of things without this supernatural reflection. Reflection: which is not the superficial, capricious game of imagining things according as we feel like it. It is easy, pleasant, comfortable to dream and imagine; but not only does it solve nothing, it turns us into lazy, spineless sluggards. The dreamer lives quite happily in that ideal world of his fancy, but reality disgusts him because in it he has to make an effort to understand and act properly. Dreamers are usually lazy, indecisive, and maladjusted; they try to escape from real life because it overwhelms them and they cannot control or direct it. Not only do they lack any interior life, but they erect an enormous barrier within themselves that prevents it ever developing, because the noise of their own inner world is so loud, so deafening, that quiet thought is impossible.

Silence is an indispensable condition for keeping things and pondering them in one's heart. Profundity of thought can develop only in a climate of silence. Too much chatter exhausts our inner strength; it dissipates everything of any value in our heart, which becomes like a bottle of perfume left open for a long time: only water remains, with a slight touch of its former fragrance. This double silence, interior and exterior, is expressed in a word often used in spiritual books, the word *recollection*. Without recollection there can be no interior life. "As long as I have strength to breathe," says St. Josemaría Escrivá, "I will continue to preach that it is vitally necessary that we be souls of prayer *at all times*, at every opportunity, and in the most varied of circumstances, for God never abandons us."[1]

Perhaps it may seem impossible to maintain such recollection in the middle of the world, especially the modern world, in which the rush and confusion, noise and speed, the ceaseless activity, the hard struggle for existence leave very little time for reflection. Nevertheless, recollection is possible and is much needed today precisely because the world

[1] J. Escrivá de Balaguer, *Friends of God*, no. 247.

is the way it is. We must remember that the Virgin Mary did not live in a convent but in the middle of the world, in a humble family whose sustenance from day to day depended on ordinary work. Speaking absolutely, it is obviously easier to practice recollection in the cloister than in the street; but let us ask ourselves whether Jesus lived an interior life of recollection during the endless activity of his public life, and whether St. Paul found it impossible. Jesus himself, by his example, shows us the method: he often went off by himself to meditate, sometimes for hours at a time. In order to be always recollected in the middle of the world with work to do, ordinary work, sometimes exhausting, we must spend some time every day *completely* alone. "Every day without fail we should devote some time especially to God, raising our minds to him, without any need for the words to come to our lips, for they are being sung in our heart. Let us give enough time to this devout practice; at a fixed hour, if possible." [2] The man who does not do this, who does not make some time to be alone and ponder in his heart those things which turn up every day, and relate them to God's plan, will never be the master of circumstances and will never profit by them. Life, like a whirlwind, will always buffet him about, he will always be the slave of impulses and passions, of actions and reactions. He will be like a withered leaf in autumn at the mercy of the winds; like a log thrown about by the rapids of a river.

Only by recollection, by keeping things, can we ponder them in our heart, and only by pondering things can we gain stability and purpose in our lives, for only then will we acquire an interior life that will direct and channel exterior events, extracting from them God's message, which is what gives them a supernatural meaning.

The spirit of poverty

What things did Mary ponder in her heart? The two times that St. Luke speaks of this interior activity he says that she

[2] *Friends of God*, no. 249.

pondered "all these words." By this he alludes to the facts that he had just narrated and that are directly related to our Lady. These facts are the birth of Jesus, the adoration of the shepherds, the presentation, the adoration of Simeon, and the episode in the Temple. Other events directly related to the Blessed Virgin are also included, although St. Luke does not record them. St. Matthew mentions, for example, the adoration of the Magi and the flight into Egypt (Mt 2:2, 13–14). In fact, the whole marvelous world that Gabriel's message opened up for her, with all its consequences and all the events connected with her Son, were subjects for meditation.

Each one of "these words" that our Lady kept and pondered opens up endless perspectives. All of them contain many lessons for us; all are full of meaning. Each of them contains a deep supernatural message that we can understand and that implicitly invites us to follow the example given.

Everything that St. Luke tells us about the Nativity is a call to poverty. The lesson, however, begins before that. There is a feast of our Lady which the Church celebrates on December 18 on which we should reflect. It is called *The Expectation of the Delivery of Our Lady*. It is a joyful preparation for the feast of the Nativity. It is easy to guess Mary's feelings during those few days immediately preceding the birth of her Son. She knew who he was to be, and all her thoughts centered on the moment when she could at last see him. The moment was near. She waited in hope, excitedly. All the Jewish people had lived for centuries with their hopes pinned on this moment; over the centuries they had been nourished with this hope. It was her Son who had been expected by one generation after another; and now all the wishes and hopes, all the trembling and emotional desire of expectancy were concentrated in her.

What mother does not dream of the child whom she is expecting? The Virgin also dreamt. Everything she had seemed very little to give him. She made plans, too, discussing them with Joseph, preparing a multitude of little details, thinking of everything, doing everything she could so that her Son, on being born, would have everything that a mother could possibly give to her newly born child. But then, when the day arrived, God simply destroyed all her plans, all her hopes and dreams. Jesus was not born in her house, not even in any house; with difficulty he found a stable, a place for animals.

There is only one type of dream that does not interfere—at least not completely—with the interior life: dreams of things within the bounds of possibility. It is very natural to make plans, to have hopes and ambitions, and it does not separate us from God or prevent us from pondering things in our heart; on the contrary, these hopes help us to fulfill the divine plan when they are based on concrete reality and aimed at definite, concrete objectives—when we dream with our feet on the ground. That is a way of applying our intelligence to the service of God, for since man is intelligent he must obey intelligently. God indicates what we should do in a general way, but he leaves a great part of our destiny to personal effort and our own initiative. It is good to make plans, to dream, to hope, but we must always be disposed to accept God's will happily, and without complaint, if he should decide to sweep all our dreams and hopes aside, as he has a perfect right to do. "For my thoughts are not your thoughts, neither are your ways my ways," says the Lord (Is 55:8). God has given us intelligence, and it is only fitting that we should have our own point of view, provided we do not forget that God, too, has his, and that when the two conflict, God is always right, because he cannot err. We make mistakes so easily and so frequently that it is amazing how slow we are to give up our opinions; it is astounding how our hearts become attached to insignificant trifles just because we thought of them ourselves, because they are "ours."

When we read of the birth of Christ in St. Luke, in spite of his reticence, we still get some idea of those anxious hours Mary spent in Bethlehem. She knew how near her delivery was. Following the edict of Augustus, many Jews of the house of David had come to Bethlehem to register, and the little village was crowded far beyond its capacity. Besides,

Mary and Joseph were poor and could not afford to pay much for a room. There was no room for them in the inn, nor in any other place. All doors were closed to them. The helplessness, the absolute misery, the complete forlornness, the total lack of those things that even the poorest of people have, the feeling of wretchedness and dire need, the terrible sadness of not being able to offer the new-born infant even a roof and walls to keep out the cold: these are heart-rending sorrows that no one, however poor, however destitute, can experience as keenly as did the Blessed Virgin, full of grace. It was as if God had abandoned his Son.

Finally, they had to go to the outskirts of Bethlehem and take refuge in a cave that was used as a stable. And there in the stable the long-awaited Messiah was born. How could the Virgin help pondering these things? God had deprived her of her dreams and hopes; he had made her endure the direst poverty, the lack of things which even the poorest of mothers have, the humiliation of having to beg for a roof and be politely but coldly refused. No one listened to her; no one was interested in her personal problem. And when the Child was born she was able to offer him only a hollow stone that was used as a manger, and perhaps a handful of straw to make it a little less hard.

For century after century the Jewish people had waited for the promised Redeemer. The prophets had spoken of him, and the leaders of the Jews, the chief priests, the doctors of the Law, the Scribes and the Pharisees all carefully guarded and transmitted the revelation. The Redeemer came, and instead of finding his people waiting for him, he found them asleep. They all were sleeping soundly on that cold night in Bethlehem, warm in their beds, in the comfort and privacy of their own homes. Suddenly, out of silence of the night, the Virgin heard voices approaching the stable; shy and happy voices, excited and hopeful. They were the voices of some poor shepherds, rough and uncouth in their ragged sheepskins, austere men, little given to laughter, with weather-worn faces and hands strong and coarse from hard work. To them God had revealed the mystery. They were the chosen few among all the men of the earth, chosen to be the first to see and adore the Christ Child, the first to smile at him, to be moved with tenderness at the sight of him, the first on whom the innocent eyes of the Child rested.

What a lovely symphony of poverty! God chose to reveal himself first to the very poorest. Is it possible that God did not love his Son? But how could he not love him, the Word, the Only-Begotten, the substantial image of the Father, God himself? Or is it possible that he did not love Mary? Equally impossible! She knew well that God loved her; she knew that she was the woman whom he had loved most, who had found grace in his eyes, the blessed among women. She knew that the love of the Father for her was unique, that nobody could ever be more loved than she. How, then, could she explain all these things? Why, if the Father loved them so much, had he surrounded them with such humility and such complete poverty? There must have been a reason for this, and there was. When someone loves, he always gives the best things he can to the beloved. God chose poverty for Jesus and his Mother. Poverty, then, must be the best thing.

* * *

This is something which the world, even those who call themselves Christians, will not admit. All these circumstances which surrounded the birth of Christ constitute a challenge to the world and to the world's greediness. Our Lord began his mission at the moment of his birth by living that virtue which he was later to preach with such unrelenting insistence: poverty, detachment from the things of the world, which "rust and moth consume, and thieves break in and steal" (Mt 6: 19); those worldly goods that enslave man and prevent him from finding happiness, like the rich young man who "went away sorrowful; for he had great possessions" (Mt 19: 22): worldly goods, which lead man's attention away from the eternal and center it on the things that pass and disappear like the weeds in the fields; which make Christians seek the pleasures of this world as if they were heathens (Mt 6: 32), and ignore the things of God; which cloud their intelligence and make them concentrate on

unessentials and neglect the only thing that is really important: the kingdom of God and his justice.

Our meditations on the subject of poverty too often remain in the realms of romance and unreality, as if it were
something fantastic, a kind of ideal or goal considered to be
a priori unattainable. What we need is fewer speeches in
praise of poverty and more serious consideration of the Gospels and of poverty itself. The Gospels are for everyone; the
words of Jesus are addressed to—and bind—us all; therefore
we are all invited to practice poverty. Our Lord's words on
the subject are very precise: "You cannot serve God and
mammon." Except that "the Pharisees, who were lovers of
money, heard all this, and they scoffed at him" (Lk 16:13–
14). A considerable number of Christians, even if they are
not very covetous or do not deride Jesus, think that to live
poverty is something for the Franciscans and religious, for
those who live in community away from the world, for those
who have a vow of poverty; they think it is also for the poor
people in the slums of big cities, but that for them personally
the thing is to improve their position, earn money, do business, make as much profit as they can, save, provide for the
future, hoard, be secure in life.

It is precisely because we think so little about poverty that
we have such hazy ideas about its true meaning. Jesus, Mary,
and Joseph lived in the world. The house at Nazareth was
not a convent but a home, with a husband, a wife, and a
child. It was a humble home, the home of a tradesman who
earned his bread by the sweat of his brow. Nevertheless, our
Lord in his parables often speaks of immensely wealthy men
who are so good that they symbolize the Father who is in
heaven: the father of the prodigal son, the master who distributed the talents, the king who prepared the wedding
feast. Other times he speaks of very rich men who are not
good but bad, as in the case of the wealthy Dives. What are
good or bad, then, are people, not things. Money is not,
morally speaking, in itself either good or bad. It is simply
something with which to buy things, something with which
to acquire the comforts of life or alleviate misery, with which
to do good or evil. Since it is only a means and not an end, it

can never be the primary object of a man's attention; rather it must be used in such a way and to such an extent as to achieve man's end.

For the rest, poverty does not necessarily mean goodness; destitution may lead to bitterness, hatred, envy, and desperation.

When we speak of poverty we usually consider it in terms of having or lacking, possessing much or little, having a secure future or living from hand to mouth; but this is a human, not a supernatural, way of looking at poverty or riches. The message of the Gospel is much deeper than that. One can have nothing and still be rich in greed, in desire of wealth and comfort; on the contrary, one can have much property and still be temperate, detached, and very generous. "True poverty is not to lack things but to be detached: to give up voluntarily one's dominion over them. That's why some poor people are really rich . . . and vice-versa."[3] The root of evangelical poverty is this detachment, this voluntary renunciation of *dominion* over things. And this is possible for everyone: for those who live in the world no less than others, for married people, for people of every walk of life and every social class.

Let us consider for a moment how absurd and out of place it would be for an actor who plays the part of a millionaire on the stage to try to keep for himself the clothes, furniture, and servants he used during his act. He would be quite mad if he thought that he was the real owner of the things that had been lent him for his part in the play. Now, the world is a great theater in which each person has his part to play, each person has some things that God lends him so that he can play his part well and properly. When the play is over, however, everything is taken away from him, because he no longer needs it. It would be just as idiotic and senseless for us to become attached to or try to have dominion over the borrowed things of the world around us as for an actor to try to use according to his own wishes the things lent to him.

Jesus was poor; he had no place to lay his head (Lk 9: 58).

---

[3] J. Escrivá de Balaguer, *The Way*, no. 632.

Nevertheless, he did not give the impression of being desti-tute. Rather, he showed himself completely uninfluenced by things, detached from them; above all, those things about which men are unusually so concerned. The explanation is this: "Don't forget it: he has most who needs least. Don't create needs for yourself." [4] The needs of Jesus—like those of Mary and Joseph—were very few. Certainly we must work hard, but our heart must always be free and detached, for greed and avarice surround us on all sides, ready to trap us. If we have faith and do whatever we can, God always gives us what we need.

Our Lady did not complain or show any sign of being annoyed with poverty; at least St. Luke says nothing about it. She had done all she could: she had knocked at every door. Then, when the Child was born, he filled her with peace and joy; his glance, his smile, his presence were so joyful that there was no time to think of anything else but him. Truly, the things of this world mean very little to those who live in the presence of God, who think of him and enjoy his peace. The heart can concentrate on only one thing at a time if it wants to possess that thing completely; that is why it is so difficult for the rich—whose heart concentrates on riches— to possess the kingdom of heaven; that is why, on the other hand, it is so easy for the poor to possess the kingdom of heaven, because they are free of these false attachments to earthly things that pass away and vanish. This explains why the woman who gave her two small coins to the Temple received such admiration and praise from Jesus: she had nothing else to give (Mk 12:41ff.). It was very little, because she was so poor. But Christ did not praise those who gave far greater sums than the widow, because they gave only part "of their abundance." Perhaps even if they had given *all* of their abundance they would have done only justice.

Everything belongs to God, heaven and earth and all that is contained therein. We are only servants, who will have to render an account of those things temporarily lent to us for the part we have to play in the world. And God is like the

[4] *The Way*, no. 630.

lord who will return from a long journey and call together his servants and ask them to give an account of what they have done with the money he has given them to do business with.

The presentiment of the cross

Eight days after his birth, according to the requirements of the Law, Christ was taken to be circumcised. He was called a name "given by the angel before he was conceived in the womb" (Lk 2: 21). Mary and Joseph, unlike Zachary, had no great celebration with all their friends because they were far away from their home and their neighbors, and they do not seem to have had any close relations in Bethlehem. Therefore there were no friends or relatives at the circumcision to interfere with the best of intentions in choosing a name for the Child. Jesus had been born with a name, his own name, and the circumcision merely served as an occasion for announcing this name to the world, making public what had up to then been known only to Mary and Joseph.

A few more weeks passed before two other precepts of the Law had to be fulfilled, in this case both being fulfilled at the same time. One of these precepts referred to the presentation. The Lord had declared to Moses that every firstborn in Israel, both man and beast, was to belong to him. Every firstborn boy should serve in God's Temple unless ransomed by the payment of a certain sum (Num 3). On payment of the proper ransom, the child was then exempt from service. The other precept concerned the mother: every woman who gave birth to a son was impure according to the law and had to stay in her house for forty days without touching anything holy; she could not enter the Temple until the time of her purification arrived. Then, after forty days, she had to go to the priest at the door of the Temple and offer a turtledove and a lamb, or two turtledoves if she was poor, which the priest in turn offered in sacrifice, praying to God for her.

When her time was fulfilled, Mary and Joseph with the Child made the journey to Jerusalem. Very humbly, like any ordinary mother, the Virgin stood with the others at the

eastern door of the Temple and waited for the priest, to give
him the doves; while Joseph waited with her to pay the
Child's ransom. They offered the Child and received him
back. Then an unexpected event occurred, which left a deep
impression on her. An old man at the door of the Temple
approached them and took the Child in his arms and began
to praise God. This old man had been promised by the Holy
Spirit that he would not die without seeing the Savior of
Israel, and it was the Spirit who now revealed the Child's
identity to him. He gave thanks to God for this great favor
and then made a revelation that gave some hint of what the
future held for this young mother and her Son. Jesus was to
be the cause of many contradictions, "set for the fall and for
the resurrection of many in Israel"; and of Mary he said:
"Thy own soul a sword shall pierce."

Even if our Lady had not been naturally predisposed by
God to contemplation and reflection, without doubt what
Simeon said during this seemingly chance and completely
unexpected meeting would have deeply impressed her. It
was a prophecy, and like all prophecies it was an incitement
to serious thought, for it contained an element of obscurity
that could not be completely understood until everything in
it was fulfilled. Those days since Jesus' birth had gone by
smoothly at Bethlehem; our Lady had been quite happy and
carefree. During the first few weeks after a child is born, the
mother is completely absorbed in taking care of it. All the
Virgin's time and care were taken up with her Child. All her
thoughts were concentrated on him.

Things might easily have continued in the same way until
Jesus began his public life. But God had other plans. At the
Annunciation God had revealed to Mary only part of his
plan of salvation. The angel Gabriel had enlightened her on
everything concerning the Incarnation of the Word, and the
part she was to play in the fulfillment of the mystery; but the
message had said nothing of how the Messiah was going to
save his people. The message dealt with the Incarnation, not
the Redemption. Whatever Mary may have known of the
bloody drama of Calvary was what she gathered from her
reading of Isaiah and one or two other scriptural references.

Undoubtedly, if the angel had told her anything else, she would have told St. Luke, as she told him about the Incarnation, and it would appear in his Gospel. But the union between mother and Son was so close, the link between them was so intimate that God—if we may use the expression—advanced the hour of that revelation. The meeting with Simeon is the moment in which she is told, not so much about the Redemption itself as about her participation in the destiny of her Son, her association with the suffering of him who was to suffer for the sins of the whole world. In like manner, later on Jesus was to prepare his disciples gradually for the Crucifixion, so that when the moment came they would not be scandalized. But he spoke to them of the Crucifixion as of something important for them, but which did not affect them personally; at most they were to be spectators, not participants. Christ's union with his disciples was not the same as his union with Mary. This gives us a brief idea of why she was enlightened in such a singular way.

Christ in his human intelligence was conscious of the Cross from an early age. It was the goal toward which he journeyed, the fulfilment of the will of the Father; it so occupied his thoughts that his heart was restless until the hour should come. God could easily have relieved the Virgin from the anguish of the knowledge that something terrible and painful was going to happen; he could have let her live happily until the moment of the Redemption came, without anything to worry about but the ordinary family cares of a poor woman. God, however, did not choose to do so. She had a presentiment of the Cross from the moment of the Presentation, just forty days after the birth of her Child. From that time on, all the happiness that Mary derived from contemplating Jesus, from seeing, hearing, and taking care of him was overshadowed by a sadness that made complete natural happiness impossible. This shadow over her life identified her even more with her Son; it brought them closer together, making them of one mind and one heart about the future Redemption, without any need for words; it joined them together in the will of the Father and set them apart from the rest of the world.

This new light exposed to her more of the depths of the great mystery: the Incarnation was the beginning of the end, the beginning of the cancellation of the debt that humanity, in Adam, had contracted to the Father. And Mary, who with her *Fiat* had surrendered herself without reserve to the will of the Father, began to see all that he expected of her; and her self-surrender grew in perfection according as her knowledge of God's plan increased.

* * *

Very likely it cannot be said that the presentiment of the Cross and the allusion to the sword that would pierce her heart embittered the life of our Lady. It is impossible to think of the Virgin Mary as a bitter person. Bitterness, in the common sense of the word, is related to discontentment; a bitter person is one who is not satisfied with his lot, who looks on life through the clouded glass of his unfortunate experience. A person who surrenders himself unconditionally to God, like our Lady, may indeed experience bitterness, a noble bitterness, but one that does not in any way change his way of life, his personality, his attitude to things. The effect of the prophecy on our Lady was probably to color her joys with a certain seriousness, a kind of gravity that prevented her from being too immersed in passing impressions or from putting her heart too much in the things of the earth.

Here also we have something to learn. By nature we tend to follow our impulses and impressions. Our whole personality is always being tugged this way and that by extremes of joy and sorrow, optimism and despair. We are always running off at loose ends after passing fancies. Joy is a virtue, but it ceases to be such when, instead of being a habit, controlled, it becomes mere self-abandonment to every instinctive reaction. We have mentioned superficiality and confusion as the result of lack of meditation and interior life. The opposite of superficiality is depth, and nothing conduces to depth so much as a "sense" of the Cross. A Christian can never live without this consciousness. The days when "philosophers" believed in the natural goodness of man and in human happiness as a consequence of progress are, fortunately, long past.

A Christian cannot, and should not, aspire to a purely natural happiness, because he is not a pagan. When he is beset with adversity he must always have hope and realize that his suffering cannot last for ever; otherwise he will be overcome by sadness and discouragement, the natural allies of sin. On the other hand, he must not completely abandon himself even to healthy joys if they are merely human; he must never give himself up entirely to the things of the moment, no matter how joyful they are. If he does, he will become immersed in the transitory and be chained to the earth, forgetting that *non habemus hic manentem civitatem*, we have not here a lasting city (Heb 13:14). The most subtle danger to the soul that this world presents is not in the clear-cut mortal sin of completely and consciously turning away from God, but in the surreptitious infiltration of a humanism whose content and limits take no account of any supernatural reality, in the enjoyment of earthly goods—however moderately—as if they were goals achieved, treating them, consciously or unconsciously, as ends in themselves. There is no Christianity without the Cross; and mortification, either willingly accepted when God sends it or undertaken voluntarily, is the normal proof that our belief in Christ is something alive and real and not merely theoretical knowledge. As we are taught in our catechism, the mark of a Christian is the sign of the Cross, and this expression is not to be limited to the mere external sign.

What we have said does not mean, however, that a Christian should lead a life of bitterness. On the contrary, if there is anything in the world that gives man a genuine joy of living it is the Gospel of Christ, the fact of being Christian. Faith in Christ makes us accept reality instead of turning our backs on it or distorting it. A true Christian can never have a hedonistic attitude to life: on the contrary, he must participate in Christ's fate and seek the Cross even in his purest and most wholesome joys.

A Christian's joys cannot be those of a healthy animal,[5] even of a superior animal. That is why the custody of the heart is so often recommended in spiritual books and so important in order for man to achieve his destiny on earth: that is, to seek Christ, to find him, to unite with him, to become another Christ. Without detachment from creatures man can never rise above them. Mortification is like a thin, very fine and delicate membrane interposed between the heart and the things of earth, preventing the heart from becoming attached to them and being kept away from God even momentarily.

Supernatural outlook

We do not know how long Mary, Joseph, and Jesus stayed in Bethlehem after the Presentation. Perhaps as soon as the registration was over they were able to get a house and leave the stable. And perhaps it was there that the Magi came; their story was astonishing, and Mary must have felt the same surprise as when Simeon took the Child in his arms in the Temple. They told of how the star appeared in the sky and guided them to Bethlehem, and of the strong desire they had to follow the star and come to adore the new-born King of the Jews. They told her how the star appeared when they arrived in Jerusalem and how Herod, the king, told them to find out where the Child was so that he too could go and adore him. And there they were, these rich and learned men, in a poor town and a humble house, kneeling before a Child, only a few months old, who was lying in his mother's lap.

That night the astonished Virgin must have gone to sleep thinking about the marvelous plans of God, moved by the faith, the simplicity, and the goodwill of those Oriental kings; she must have been extremely happy, too, at the honor being paid to her Son. Her sleep was suddenly interrupted by Joseph: they had to leave immediately. An angel had brought him a message in a dream saying: "Rise, and take the child and his mother, and flee to Egypt: and remain there

---

[5] *The Way*, no. 659.

till I tell you; for Herod is about to search for the child, to destroy him" (Mt 2:13). Another moment of happiness had suddenly vanished! What a way God treated her! Her night's sleep was interrupted to be given an unpleasant message, one which filled her with fear and anguish. Herod was so powerful, and they were so poor and insignificant! What harm had the Child done to anyone? How could Herod hate him without even knowing him?

Preparations were made to leave without a moment's delay. They had very little to take with them. Joseph "rose and took the child and his mother by night, and departed to Egypt" (Mt 2:14). They left immediately, by night, without hesitation or delay. They left in a hurry for fear delay might cost the precious life of the Child.

It was a long, tiring journey over hundreds of miles of rough, uneven paths across the desert. It was a long time before they could feel safe and out of reach of the enemy. And at the end of the journey lay a strange and unknown country, very different from everything that was familiar to them: their fields and mountains, their customs and beliefs. It cannot have been a pleasant journey, or full of the pleasant surprises that the apocryphal gospels describe: palm trees bowing in mute adoration as they passed by, ferocious bandits who suddenly change into tender, solicitous, and kind protectors, fountains springing up miraculously in the desert to quench the thirst of the humble travelers. On the contrary, we can only believe that it was the same for the Holy Family as for other travelers of the time: an exhausting trip, fatiguing, monotonous, little rest. So once again the journey to Egypt was made by the chosen ones of God, like Abraham and Joseph, like Jacob and the patriarchs.

In Egypt they had to start a new life all over again. Probably they went to some city in the north and got in contact with a Jewish colony, relying on the racial bonds to find help and make new friends. They were in a country with a different mentality and different customs, a country of idolaters. The angel's instructions had been both concrete and vague: "Remain there till I tell you." That was very clear, but Joseph had no idea of how long he would have to remain there.

Whenever anything is indefinite it is uncomfortable. This uncertainty was in itself enough to make their stay difficult. Whatever one does for an indefinite period, which may be very short or very long, runs the risk of being provisional, and anything provisional is never satisfactory. Transients can never enjoy themselves for long, for they know that everything around them will soon be left behind; and to get attached to things is even worse, because then the moment of departure is painful and sorrowful. Therefore, we must do our work as if we were going to remain in a certain place permanently, and yet at the same time we should keep ourselves detached from the things around us, as if we were to leave them the next day. There is nothing worse than a permanently provisional state.

The flight into Egypt must have engraved itself vividly in Mary's mind. However much she tried, she could hardly forget an event that changed her whole life as much as that precipitous flight into a strange, distant land, especially when she had to stay there for an indefinite time. And it is this episode more than any other that helps us to understand the normal attitude of our Lady to all the events, great and small, that went to make up her life.

* * *

We have frequently used the expression "supernatural outlook" as the contrary of what we could call "natural outlook." Natural outlook makes us consider things limited to the natural sphere, without any consideration of the world of grace, without any consideration of anything higher than what we see. Supernatural outlook, on the contrary, relates everything to God's plan, puts into practice the knowledge of God's will, which wishes or permits and disposes everything that happens in the universe. If man is always aware of the will of God, not as something dead or indifferent to the things that happen, but as an active force in the world, then he can look beyond himself and not despair or become depressed when seeming catastrophes strike him. "Perhaps the best way to picture the whole process is to visualize God, not merely creating the beginning of the world, and leaving it, so to speak, to work out its own destiny, but rather choosing this particular world with its complete history right down to the very end, after examining every single action of every single creature in full detail and in all its consequences, comparing this possible history and sequence with all other possible ones, and finally deciding to create *this* particular scheme of things in which *this* particular event, and all its consequences occur."[6]

When we look at things in this way, each occurrence, great or small, joyful or sorrowful, is no longer a full stop beyond which nothing can be done, which is final and irremediable; rather it becomes one link in a chain of which all the previous links were chosen of the very best quality.

Perhaps an example will help to clarify the difference between natural and supernatural outlook. Let us imagine for a moment that during a game of chess suddenly each piece acquires a degree of intelligence proportionate to its importance and the way in which the rules allow it to move: the queen first, then the rooks and the bishops, all the way down to the pawns. One of the players moves a pawn one space forward, which leaves the king unprotected, prevents the queen from moving, and leaves the pawn itself unprotected. This pawn, with its tiny intelligence and short sight, which barely sees beyond its own square, would think that such a move was ridiculous; if it were capable of feeling it would be upset, irritated, impatient, and unhappy. The poor pawn does not realize that the player sees not only him but all the other pieces, his own and his opponent's and, besides, is thinking of several moves ahead. With its narrow and limited intelligence, the pawn does not know that this move, which he considers disastrous, is indispensable for a checkmate that will come ten moves later.

We are like the pawns in an exciting game of chess, whose chess board is the universe and whose pieces are innumerable. God is the player, the One who foresees the movements of all the pieces; and he always wins, although to our

---

[6] Eugene Boylan, *This Tremendous Lover*, chap. 2.

poor pawn's intelligence it may seem that he slips up and makes disastrous moves.

We have a human outlook when we forget that we are pawns, when we forget that behind all those things which annoy and irritate us; which make us impatient, upset, depressed; which discourage us or fill us with a disorderly optimism, there is *something* that gives them a definite purpose. Just as a purely human outlook results in our becoming irritated and disgusted with the way life treats us, supernatural outlook leads to serenity and hope, for "to them that love God all things work together unto good" (Rom 8: 28). This supernatural vision provides us with shelter from disturbing anxieties, keeps us well-balanced and objective as between exaltation and dejection, armed with an interior calm that remains unruffled even in the presence of our own or our neighbor's miseries. As St. Josemaría Escrivá has put it: "We must not forget that for a child of God over and above the raging storm there is a sun that shines brightly and beneath the pounding and devastating waves there is a prevailing stillness and calm." Now, then, we need faith in order to see beyond the superficial appearances of things: faith in God and in the word of God. Supernatural outlook is simply living our faith every day in the most insignificant details of our existence.

If our Lady had viewed life from a purely natural point of view, she would have had more than sufficient reasons to be upset. For, if God were omnipotent, why did he not spare his Son that danger? Why did he burden the Holy Family with the anguish of the flight into Egypt and the misery of living in a strange country? Why did he disrupt the peaceful course of their lives with such a journey? It would have been easy for him to make Herod die a little sooner, or else change his evil designs. But instead, God permitted the violent deaths of innocent children who had nothing to do with Herod or Jesus, and all the resulting sorrow to their mothers.

Mary, however, pondered these things in her heart. She did not understand them, at least some of them, but she knew that God was behind everything and that what she did not understand had its explanation in God. She did not ask for miracles, but respected the mysterious wishes of the Creator; she knew the power of human liberty, she knew that sin existed. Her Son was concerned precisely with these things. He had come to repair the damage man had done by sin and the misuse of his freedom. God knew what value these things, which from the human viewpoint were real catastrophes, had in relation to eternal life.

As St. Matthew remarks, another prophecy had been fulfilled: "Out of Egypt have I called my son" (Mt 2:15). God uses man's actions, always respecting his free will, to fulfill his designs. In this case he used Herod's evil plan to fulfill the prophecy; just as he had used the emperor's census as a starting point for a series of events that ended in the fulfillment of another prophecy—and Jesus was born in Bethlehem when everything pointed logically to his being born in Nazareth. This is the wonderful thing about God's action in the world: without forcing anyone or anything, he makes of everything an instrument of his glory for the good of those who love him. It is of no importance that sometimes—or many times—that good is not the good we would have liked; it is enough for us to know that he makes no mistakes and that he always wins, so that nothing—no event, no person—can make us lose our serenity and peace; for God can right everything that seems wrong and save everything that seems lost. As long as we are limited by our own smallness, our observation is restricted to what we see—which is not much—and the world frequently appears to be woven of events whose meaning we do not perceive. "Here," Chesterton reminds us through one of his most famous characters, Father Brown, "we live on the wrong side of the tapestry . . . ; the things that happen here have no meaning whatsoever; but later on, elsewhere, everything becomes meaningful." True enough, now we can see only the wrong side of the tapestry, only what is human and all the imperfections that it entails; one has to go round to "the other side" in order to see things in their entirety: the part we contribute and the action of God, human imperfection utilized, corrected, made whole by grace.

Naturalness and discretion

Although our Lady's permanent attitude was one of profound contemplation, we must not think that she lived an inactive life. To be a contemplative does not at all mean to be inactive. The fact that she pondered in her heart all the things she observed, not only those which affected her directly but also those which happened around her, did not prevent her from living her own life with complete naturalness within the environment and under the conditions in which God had placed her.

St. Luke and St. Matthew give an account of certain events that affected her very closely. They were not ordinary, but extraordinary, happenings, which stand out above those which normally befall most of us; that is why they were recorded. They must have impressed our Lady very deeply: that is why she told St. Luke about them. But obviously Mary's entire life was not a succession of such extraordinary events. The fact that the evangelists say nothing about the rest of Mary's life indicates that there was nothing else to say, that the other details of her life were trivial, commonplace, and very ordinary. And it is precisely this lack of information, the fact that the evangelists say nothing, that leads us to certain considerations of incalculable value.

First of all, as far as we know, there was nothing outstanding in the life of the Virgin except the things mentioned by the evangelists. Nazareth was a small village, and a carpenter named Joseph lived in a very humble house and supported his family by working hard. Mary was the wife of this carpenter. She did the same things as any other poor man's wife. She was a housewife, always busy with the hundred little things to be done around the house, monotonously repeated day after day and year after year; the same things that fill the lives of so many other women.

The second consideration has already been concisely expressed with great clarity and precision in *The Way*: "Mary most holy, Mother of God, passes unnoticed, just as one more among the women of her town. Learn from her how to live with 'naturalness'."[7] Let us leave any consideration of this for the moment and try to penetrate a little further into this aspect of Mary's life.

So far as external appearances are concerned, there seems to have been nothing conspicuous or remarkable about our Lady to set her apart from other women. It is true that a shrewd observer would have noticed something distinctive in her dignified and serene bearing, and that those who came in contact with her could not fail to be captivated by her sweetness and tenderness, her depth and simplicity. Anyone who has an interior life and a strong, harmonious personality can never be confused with superficial and mediocre people. Interior delicacy and spiritual elegance cannot fail to influence a person's behavior, gestures, conversation, and smile. But that is not what we mean here. We are considering Mary's dress, manners, language, and customs, which were all exactly the same as those of the women around her. The shepherds found a young and happy mother and her child in the stable, with nothing to indicate that she was the mother of the Messiah. The Magi found a young woman simply clothed in ordinary Jewish dress, with the Child on her lap, and there was nothing in her appearance or clothes that could have revealed to them that she was the most blessed among all women, immeasurably superior in dignity and majesty to all the queens and great ladies in the world. When she was at the eastern gate of the Temple with the Child in her arms, waiting with many other mothers to present the Child and be purified herself, in the eyes of any onlooker she was just another mother. Simeon did not discover her directly; he discovered Jesus and through Jesus he discovered her.

The people of Nazareth, her neighbors, never knew who was living among them, with whom they were associating. They never knew that Mary, the wife of Joseph the carpenter, was the Mother of the God-Man. Mary herself never disclosed the secret of her Son, nor did she take advantage of the privileges that were hers because of her great dignity.

[7] *The Way*, no. 499.

She never let anyone know, either directly or indirectly, her superiority, her greatness. Except at Cana, when she did what she had to do and then discreetly mingled in the crowd, we never see her near Jesus in the moments when the enthusiastic multitudes acknowledged him as Messiah and wished to proclaim him king. "Mary most holy, Mother of God, passes unnoticed, just as one more among the women of her town. Learn from her how to live with 'naturalness'." [8] "Mary, teacher of the sacrifice that is hidden and silent. See her, nearly always in the background, cooperating with her Son: she knows and remains silent." [9] "What humility, that of my holy Mother Mary! She's not to be seen amidst the palms of Jerusalem, nor—except that first one at Cana—at the hour of the great miracles. But she doesn't flee from the degradation of Golgotha: there she stands, *juxta crucem Jesu,* 'by the cross of Jesus'—his Mother." [10]

It is surely remarkable that when Jesus proclaimed himself Messiah those who had lived with him in the same village for many years were scandalized and excused their disbelief by saying that he was the son of Mary: "Is not this the carpenter, the son of Mary?" (Mk 6: 3).

Any attempt to understand, with our normal mentality, the position of the Virgin Mary in relation to the environment and people with whom she lived will be very difficult. Franz Willam has written some penetrating pages which, happily, do much to destroy that idea we often have that everything went smoothly and easily for our Lady; the pages refer primarily to the time of the Incarnation but can be equally applied to her hidden life. The world hates to admit anything beyond its understanding. From an extraordinary being the world expects extraordinary things, and the Virgin did nothing extraordinary. Satan himself tempted Jesus to make himself known by performing something spectacular: "If you are the Son of God, throw yourself down" (Mt 4: 6). The world, the contemporaries of Jesus and Mary, expected wonders and signs that would fit

[8] *The Way*, no. 499.
[9] *The Way*, no. 509.
[10] *The Way*, no. 507.

in with their own way of imagining the Messiah; the world is the same now as it was then. Many people today wish from the bottom of their hearts that some extraordinary, astounding event would happen and put an end to all corruption, disbelief, ill will: in short, evil itself. Perhaps even if something like this did happen, the results would be the same as those in Bruce Marshall's novel, when Father Malachy miraculously transported a scandalous cabaret from in front of a Catholic church to a solitary rock off the coast of Scotland: as soon as the people got over their initial surprise, and the sensation died down, everything went on as before; the good continued to be good, and the bad continued to be bad. The only person who profited from the miracle was the owner of the cabaret, whose fame was spread by the enormous free publicity and the sensation caused by the whole thing. The fact is, as Moeller says, that if a man is not morally disposed to seek God, he will not be converted even by the most sensational miracles. Undoubtedly the Son of God performed many miracles, openly and clearly, but the Jews were not converted. When they saw the resurrection of Lazarus, who had been rotting in the tomb, all they concluded was that Jesus had to die (Jn 11:47ff.).

This thick, impenetrable wall of narrow minds must have caused the Blessed Virgin much suffering. The fact that she did not try to stand out among those around her, to impress them or to persist in continuous and useless arguments to make people recognize her true dignity and superiority, made it possible for her to live quietly among the Jews, influencing them, fulfilling her mission and helping Jesus to fulfill his: by being so natural she was even more effective than John the Baptist, who had been expressly created by God to prepare the way of the Lord. She accepted the world as it was, as her Son accepted it. Her naturalness certainly contributed in no small measure to the fulfillment of God's plan: she never made a fuss about anything she did, she never wished to shine or be noticed. She always carried out the will of God and never consulted her own opinions except in those things God left to her own initiative. And the thing that enabled the Virgin to pass unnoticed through life with absolute naturalness was her discretion.

In times like these, when journalism, love of news and gossip, publicity and advertising dominate our society like gods that think they have the right to oust all privacy, there are not many people who understand the meaning of discretion. Curiosity on the one hand and the desire of notoriety on the other join together to discredit the virtue of discretion and to erase even the memory of its name: discretion is now being treated as mystery or secrecy. The virtue of discretion consists in not telling people what does not concern them; in not broadcasting what should be sheltered from curious ears and inquisitive eyes; in not making an exhibition of things that are private and intimate; in not putting in the foreground what should be in the background. Discretion is prudence in speech and in action, and we can learn much about discretion by meditating on the example of our Lady.

She never revealed to anyone the great mystery of her maternity; this mystery remained pure and uncontaminated, untouched by the materialism of worldly life, while at the same time it filled the life of the Virgin with its fragrance and influenced every act of her daily work. Everyone is what he is and everyone acts in accordance with what he thinks of himself: a man acts as a man, the violent act violently, the saints as saints. The fact that Mary was the Mother of God did not make her famous in her own time; on the contrary, it changed nothing of the circumstances in which she lived her ordinary life; she was still the wife of a poor carpenter, surrounded by the same friends she had always had in Nazareth, subject to the same obligations as if she were not the most privileged among women. God changed nothing of her external life, nothing of her surroundings, when the Word became flesh; and she, who was always faithful, did nothing to change what God had not changed; she had no wish to use the spiritual gifts for material gain; she had no wish to put supernatural privileges at the service of earthly goals.

Unquestionably, the best way to appear like something is

to be it. Nevertheless, we sometimes do not take the trouble of being what we want everyone to think we are. Very few people like to pass through life unnoticed. It is true that our Lord said: "Let your light so shine before men, that they may see your good works and give glory to your Father who is in heaven" (Mt 5: 16). What we should notice here is that he never said: *Make sure* that your light shines before men. Our objective should never be to shine; instead we should put all our efforts in having light, because shining is then simply a consequence. Besides, a light does not place itself on a candlestick—it has to be placed there; if we have any light, God will see to it that we are placed where our light is needed. This can also be applied to the world and our environment. Each of us should be known for his works; people frequently shine in the world, not for their works, but by a swindle: behind all the publicity they get there is nothing but a photograph, a journalist friend, or nothing at all. If a man does things in order to shine, while in fact he has no light, the result is lack of naturalness, artificiality, strangeness, oddity: publicity and propaganda. To do some thing merely to attract attention is despicable; from the human point of view despicable, and from the supernatural point of view sterile: "Truly, I say to you, they have their reward" (Mt 6: 2).

It is even worse to use the spiritual to obtain material benefits, or to endanger our own spiritual life by making an exhibition, without discretion or control, of the things that belong solely to our intimate life with God, *in order to* "give good example." Do you think that the Virgin or Christ did things *in order to* give good example? To give good example is a consequence of doing good; it is not an end in itself. The only end we should ever have is to do the the will of the Father. To "play to the gallery," as if we were on a stage, takes away all authenticity, because it is not the result of interior overflowing but merely an artificial pose adopted to suit the world or the moment; when we adopt such a pose in relation to supernatural things, we bring about a basic contradiction which eventually destroys our personality, the foundation of our very being. "I like Catholics to carry

Christ not in name, but in their conduct, giving a real witness of Christian life. I find clericalism repellent and I understand how, as well as an evil anticlericalism, there also
exists a healthy anticlericalism. It proceeds from love for the
priesthood and opposes the use of a sacred mission for
earthly ends, either by a layman or by a priest." [11]

Our Lady obeyed the law by presenting herself at the
temple to be purified, although she had no need of purification; she did not want to use her privileges in order to be
exempt from the common precept that all mothers had to
observe. On the other hand, we must not think that in order
to avoid attention the Virgin ever did anything that was not
correct, or that she omitted even the slightest of her duties
simply because the atmosphere was not favorable. Without
doubt, some of our Lady's opinions and action surprised
those around her, until they got used to her attitude, if they
ever did. It is natural that, since she was so different, there
should be some trace of this difference reflected in her way
of acting, some mark of her unique personality, but this was
something that flowed unintentionally from within her.
Naturalness consists not so much in making great efforts to
avoid attention, as in behaving as we are, doing what we
should do in whatever situation or environment we happen
to be even if that attracts attention; for it is not a matter of
hiding or disguising anything, or of deceiving in order to
avoid the limelight.

No one can fail to notice the supreme naturalness of our
Lord during the years of his public life; and yet he did things
that attracted attention—his miracles—and astonished
those around him, but still he did not stop. And yet he did
even these things with complete naturalness, that is to say,
without ostentation, without giving them more importance
than any other act, because for him it was as easy to raise the
dead and heal the sick as to do the work of a carpenter or to
speak to little children.

In the world of today, discretion and naturalness are two
virtues that every Christian should possess and cultivate, for

[11] J. Escrivá de Balaguer, *Conversations*, no. 47.

only thus can he be the leaven in the bread, that is, in the world around him. "Naturalness. Let your Christian spirit—your salt and your light—be manifested spontaneously, without anything odd or foolish. Always carry with you your spirit of simplicity." [12] Only if he possesses these virtues can a Christian fulfill his duties in the middle of the world, because only then can he demonstrate that life and religion are not incompatible, that there is no reason why they should be separated, and that, on the contrary, religion gives meaning and purpose to life. The contemporary world, with all its difficulties, is no more unfavorable to Christians than that of pagan Rome, Corinth, or Ephesus in the first centuries of our era; and the first Christians were able to live in peace with their neighbors without any apparent differences, but at the same time without any compromises that would betray their own vocation.

The value of little things

Our Lady spent the greater part of her life doing things that were so ordinary and common that it is impossible to give the history of them. They have no special history because they are common to everyone; such small and insignificant acts that, if they were written down, they would constitute the biography of countless persons. St. Luke does not mention these things because they are not worth mentioning; nevertheless, his very silence should incite us to think about them. [13]

In the main our Lady's life was like the lives of most of us: the same things happened to her as to us. She did not perform any miracles while she was on earth. Except for the Annunciation, the coming of the Magi, and the adoration of the shepherds, there was nothing in her life exteriorly extraordinary; and even these were not things that she did but that were done to her. If we glance through any history book it is very easy to find persons whose lives were much more outstanding, men who did truly extraordinary

[12] *The Way*, no. 379.
[13] See J. Escrivá de Balaguer, *Christ Is Passing By*, no. 148.

deeds and performed tremendous feats: saints and kings, soldiers and heroes. Nevertheless, without having performed great deeds, the fact is that our Lady is far above all these saints and kings, soldiers and heroes; she is greater than the greatest characters in history. Her life is marked by an uncommon grandeur, and in this she is indeed extraordinary.

Her normal occupation was work—ordinary, everyday tasks. She was a poor, simple woman whose work consisted of all those small chores around the house; cooking, cleaning the house, baking bread, going for water, washing clothes, and so forth. Her friends were neither very many nor very remarkable: other women, other families, as poor and simple as herself, of her own social class, her neighbors. Their conversation was about the countless trivial and uninteresting happenings that occur in a small and isolated village. All in all, these petty, insignificant things are hardly worthy of attention, nothing extraordinary.

Nevertheless, the Virgin Mary is the most holy of creatures, and holiness requires heroic virtues, great fidelity to grace, and complete correspondence with the inspirations of the Holy Spirit. The Virgin, as we know, from the first moment in which she was created, had more grace than all the saints put together, but her sanctity did not consist solely in this. All through her life her sanctity continually grew, increasing with every moment of time. There were certain moments when her faith, fortitude, and charity increased tremendously, that is when she was confronted with situations which required a great effort. But such situations, as we have said, were only rare moments in her life, and in general her sanctity increased, not in bursts, but slowly, day by day. There must be some value in these dull, ordinary, little everyday tasks, seeing that the Virgin did not disdain to spend almost her whole life doing such things, and that they were the main occupation of that just man Joseph, and especially seeing that Christ himself spent eighteen years of his life doing them.

It is a well-known fact that sanctity, perfection, does not consist in doing great and extraordinary deeds. It may or may not consist of such deeds because it is distinct and does not depend on the greatness of the things done. What we should stress here is that little things have a value that cannot be despised; if we do so we run the risk of losing not only our chances of perfection—which becomes impossible—but even of losing our souls. To put it very simply: most Christians—in fact, the great majority—will never have any occasion during the whole of their lives to do great things for God or for the Church; since they have no chance of doing great things, if they do not want to do the small things, what, then, can they do? [14]

Many times we have insisted on the radical difference between appearances and reality. If we watch a military parade, there is nothing more difficult than to tell one soldier from another; they all have the same uniform and all take the same steps and all go through the same gestures; yet there may be a saint marching beside a sinner, an illiterate man beside a man of great culture, an idiot beside a man of clear-sighted intelligence. It is difficult to tell one little thing from another: they may be the same in appearance and yet completely different. Two men in a factory can both make the same effort, and yet the work of one will be perfect and the work of the other defective, although to an onlooker there may be no difference.

Greatness and sanctity consist not in *what* one does but in *how* one does it. What ultimately gives quality to our actions is the love, the energy, the perfection with which we perform them. Some actions require hardly a second of decision: great deeds can often be the fruit of mere emotion, impulse, and excitement. But what is really difficult, what demands courage above the ordinary—although *everyone* can attain it—what requires great resolution and continuous effort is daily perseverance in doing well the monotonous tasks that have to be done day after day. It is not particularly admirable to go to the office every day, but it is most admirable to go there every day at nine o'clock, and, as Kipling says, to fill every inexorable minute of sixty seconds with hard work,

[14] *Christ Is Passing By*, nos. 37, 44, 77, 148, and so on; *The Way*, nos. 814–830.

without allowing laziness, boredom, or even fatigue to mar the quality of that work.

It is encouraging for us to know our Lady achieved her incomparable sanctity through these small, everyday actions. All our life, so ordinary, so monotonous, made up of little joys and unimportant sorrows, of commonplace occupations and happenings, can become something very great if we do everything for love, with enthusiasm and trying for perfection. A little thing like fixing a pillow for a sick person can be completely different, depending on whether it is done by a mother or a stranger. We think we have to be especially careful about only big things, but that is because of a distorted sense of values, which measures things according to the effort we have to expend in doing them, or the admiration that they arouse in others. Greatness, according to this criterion, would depend on accidental circumstances, and we would have to deny any greatness to the Virgin because nobody could say that taking care of the Child or the house demanded great effort or aroused great admiration.

It is very significant that the lord in the parable rewards his servant *quia super pauca fuistis fidelis*, because "you have been faithful over little things" (Mt 25:21), and that Christ himself says: "He who is faithful in a very little is faithful also in much; and he who is dishonest in a very little is also dishonest in much" (Lk 16:10). Our Lady's decisive *fiat* in the most important moment of her life, when an extraordinary degree of faith, hope, and charity were demanded of her, would be impossible without the preparation of the years that preceded it, years in which nothing special happened, but during which her faithfulness in the countless minute details of her everyday life prepared her for the moment when God asked of her something great. In the same way her strength at the foot of the Cross, her closeness to her Son when he was humiliated and condemned to death, was made possible only by her union with him throughout the preceding years. Faithfulness in great trials is determined by faithfulness in little things. No great discovery is made without many years of obscure work, constant efforts, many hours spent in apparently fruitless experiments. It is the same way with anything else in life. "Have you seen how that imposing building was constructed? One brick after another. Thousands. But, one by one. And bags and bags of cement, one by one. And stone upon stone, each of them insignificant compared with the massive whole. And beams of steel, and men working, hour after hour, day after day . . .

"Did you see how that imposing building was constructed? . . . By dint of little things!" [15]

To reach a million—in anything—we have to begin with one, then two, then three . . . until we reach the million. No one wins important athletic contests without previous training that extends to everything in the athlete's life: moderation in eating and drinking, breathing exercises, and so many hours of daily workouts. Success depends on the way in which the previous training was done. In the same way: "'Great' holiness consists in carrying out the 'little' duties of each moment." [16]

The contrary is also true. No great spiritual or material catastrophe comes from nothing. Ascetical theology has made detailed studies of that phenomenon in the spiritual life called *lukewarmness*, which is characterized especially by contempt of little things. It is terrible to think where such a state logically leads: not only to the death of a soul, but to total dryness in the sources of the soul's vitality so that it prevents any rebirth of spiritual life. Great falls are brought about, sometimes over a very long period, by a person letting himself drift into a habit of carelessness, which cause many small falls; the soul becomes accustomed to giving in easily and taking the line of least resistance, letting itself be dragged along by whatever is most pleasant. Great cowardice is the result of little acts of cowardice every day, for one cannot conquer in the big things if one does not want to conquer in the little things. [17]

The explanation of the enormous value of little things is

[15] *The Way*, no. 823.
[16] *The Way*, no. 817.
[17] See *The Way*, no. 828.

to be found in what we might call the mechanics of sanctity. Sanctity is union with God, and union with God consists in doing his will always and in everything. The will of God for us is, like God himself, permanent—there is no real distinction between God and his attributes; it is inconceivable that God would want something from us at certain times of the day or on certain days of the year and then forget about us the rest of the time, leaving us to our own whims. Sleeping, eating, thinking, all these things are the will of God; he has created us with a nature that requires these functions. We can either allow these natural functions to divert us from or lead us to God; either we can be disorderly and capricious, following solely our own whims, or we can use our faculties when and how God wants them to be used. When we are unfaithful even to those slight promptings of grace that urge us to avoid disorder and give God his due, this unfaithfulness weakens us and makes it more difficult for us to accept all the graces that God has prepared for us. All graces are closely related; that is why little infidelities lead us to great disasters; that is why the same small daily actions can either unite us to God or slowly separate us from him for ever; that is why sanctity centers on perfection in little things because "everything in which we poor little men take part—even sanctity—is a fabric of small trifles which, depending upon one's intention, can form a splendid tapestry of heroism or of degradation, of virtue or of sin." [18]

The tapestry of our Lady's sanctity was not made up of three or four masterly threads on a background of nothing or insipidity. In a perfect picture even the most insignificant line is perfect; one imperfect line leaves an imperfect whole. The most admirable thing in the life of our Lady, and the thing that everyone can imitate, is without doubt her hidden life, her fidelity in little things, her perfection in things that are invisible to everyone except God. This was the normal means Mary had at her disposal for giving expression to her great love for God; when someone is in love he puts his heart into everything he does, making it a

[18] *The Way*, no. 826.

testimony of his love. St. Augustine says that when someone is in love there is no work, and if there is, it is also loved, because every act and gesture of one who is in love bears the mark of his love.[19]

---

[19] See J. Escrivá de Balaguer, *Christ Is Passing By*, no. 148.

5

CANA

On the third day there was a marriage at Cana in Galilee, and the mother of Jesus was there; Jesus also was invited to the marriage, with his disciples. When the wine failed, the mother of Jesus said to him, "They have no wine." And Jesus said to her, "O woman, what have you to do with me? My hour has not yet come." His mother said to the servants, "Do whatever he tells you." Now six stone jars were standing there, for the Jewish rites of purification, each holding twenty or thirty gallons. Jesus said to them, "Fill the jars with water." And they filled them up to the brim. He said to them, "Now draw some out, and take it to the steward of the feast." So they took it. When the steward of the feast tasted the water now become wine, and did not know where it came from (though the servants who had drawn the water knew), the steward of the feast called the bridegroom and said to him, "Every man serves the good wine first; and when men have drunk freely, then the poor wine; but you have kept the good wine until now." This, the first of his signs, Jesus did at Cana in Galilee, and manifested his glory; and his disciples believed in him.

JOHN 2:1–11

Social life

One day an extraordinary rumor began to circulate in Palestine. Beside the Jordan a man had started preaching a baptism of penance, saying that the kingdom of God was at hand. He was a strange man, strong and very austere, gifted with a tremendous personality and forceful inner power that drew people from all over the country to him as if he were a magnet. They came from many towns and villages,

173

including Nazareth, and on returning home, of course, made many comments about this new prophet and his preaching. And one day Jesus, perhaps with many others from the town, also went to see him. He had already begun his public life and was just thirty years old. His mother was left at home, alone.

Not long afterward, Mary received an invitation to a wedding that was taking place in Cana, Galilee. A wedding in Palestine and among the Jews was an important event and took the form of a religious ceremony, for it was the means of perpetuating the race until the fullness of time, that is, until the coming of the Messiah. The bride and groom were friends, perhaps relatives, of hers, so Mary accepted the invitation and went to Cana. Jesus and his disciples were also invited and once again, although for a short time, Mother and Son were reunited.

The preaching of John the Baptist had been the topic of many comments, and it is possible that, among these comments, there had been some talk of how the young prophet testified to Jesus. Furthermore, our Lord had already begun to gather some disciples about him who recognized him as their Master. We do not know if Jesus had yet been publicly identified as the Messiah, awaited for so many centuries; but undoubtedly at the time of this wedding he had gained some fame, which made him a very different and superior personage to all the guests, superior also to the carpenter of Nazareth, as he had been known by everyone: the very fact that he was invited *with his disciples* indicates this. Besides, Nathanael was from Cana, and it is very probable that he had told the others how and why he had become a disciple of Jesus.

Perhaps because there were too many guests or because of a miscalculation, the time came when the wine began to run short and it became obvious that there would not be enough for the rest of the wedding feast. This was a serious thing because it would leave an unhappy memory of their wedding in the minds of the bride and groom and would be the subject of much unfavorable gossip in the town for a long time. And then, before anyone noticed the scarcity, our Lady intervened.

It seems probable that she was not content to enjoy the general gaiety of the feast or to listen with a mother's natural pride to the things that everyone was saying about her Son. The fact that she realized so quickly that the wine was running out makes us think that she was discreetly concerned with the comfort of the guests, perhaps helping—although certainly without interfering—in the tasks that were the business of the steward. The fact is that as soon as she realized the wine was running short she tried to think of a way to remedy the situation. It is possible, as Franz Willam points out, that she understood the significance of the fact that Jesus had been recognized as the Messiah, even if only by his disciples, and perhaps she thought that the time had come for him to reveal himself publicly as the Messiah, and that was why she came to him, asking for a solution to the problem, at the same time offering herself as a collaborator or mediatrix. This might explain Jesus' answer: "His hour" had not yet come; he did not need her collaboration, thus intimating perhaps that when it did come she could collaborate with him.

On the other hand, however, perhaps the things happened much more simply. When the Virgin noticed the lack of wine she thought of the embarrassment it would cause the young couple. Her kindness made her feel sorry for them and wonder how she could help them. But what could she do in such a situation? She could thank of no solution. And with absolute naturalness she told her Son what was troubling her: "They have no wine."

Jesus' reply recalls his answer to another question of hers eighteen years previously in the Temple at Jerusalem, and the remarks made about that episode should be recalled here. For here also Jesus makes the distinction between the Son of Mary and the Son of God. Mary made a request of Jesus as her Son, but Jesus answered her as the Messiah: he had not come to solve material problems; his mission was that given to him by the Father. Once he had made this fact clear, he did not hesitate to make his hour come—the hour to perform a miracle that would manifest his power and give testimony of his divinity.

Mary, however, was very wise. Interior reflection on all the things that she had seen and that had happened to her had made her grow in faith and wisdom. Jesus' reply is surprising, but Mary's reaction is even more so. We do not know whether Jesus said anything more than what St. John recorded, but it is reasonable to think that the dialogue between Jesus and his Mother was not confined to such a curt request and answer. Certainly Jesus could not be indifferent to a beseeching, trusting, loving glance from Mary. In any case, we know that she acted with complete self-confidence, as if she knew what she was doing. She approached the servants, perhaps hired merely for this feast, and gave them very simple instructions: "Whatever he shall say to you, do ye." Then the Virgin mingled with the guests again just as before.

* * *

As St. John observes, this miracle at Cana was the first that Jesus performed, but as well as being the first it was also the most joyful. And he performed it at the request of the Virgin Mary, so that the wedding feast might continue and the happiness of the young couple not be disturbed. The fact that the Virgin and Jesus himself attended the marriage feast, in the first place, indicates that there are certain social obligations which, because they are obligations, must be fulfilled. Man is sociable by nature. He cannot live alone, and so true is this that even the first hermits who went to live in the deserts ended up living in communities, thus opening the way for the later monasteries. Only by exception can a man live isolated, for no one can fulfill his mission fully outside the community, apart from society.

It is, then, a consequence of human nature itself that there should be a whole series of links that bind men to other men in mutual interdependence, which, in turn, obliges them to unite. This is just another phenomenon of everyday life that, like all the others, can either lead us to God or constitute an obstacle to keep us from him. It all depends on the intention behind our relations with people, on the attitude we adopt to them, on how we deal with them. No Christian either can, or should, in any way evade these obligations which derive from his very nature and are imposed on him by the mere fact that he lives among other men. This was probably neither the first nor the last marriage that the Virgin and Jesus attended, for while they were in Nazareth, a small town in which everyone knew everyone else and everybody was at home in everybody else's house, there must have been many small social events that Jesus and Mary had to attend. We know for certain that during his public life our Lord attended social gatherings that were not of such a religious character as a wedding, sometimes to the great scandal of the Jews. Jesus accepted invitations to attend banquets; for instance, one given by Matthew, which was attended by his publican friends, who were considered sinners by most Jews; and one given by a Pharisee; and another by Simon the leper and another by Lazarus in Bethany. We also know that our Lord had friends: for instance, the small family of Martha, Mary, and Lazarus, in whose house he often stayed the night. Other times our Lord did not even wait for a formal invitation but invited himself, as he did in Jericho when he went to the house of Zacheus.

Therefore, far from being bad, it is very good to attend to our social obligations. And, since it is good, we should not just tolerate them but rather cultivate them, not as if we were making a great sacrifice and suffering agony, but with the happy heart of one who shares something with other children of God, one who is enriched and matured by contact with others. A Christian must never use the pretext of asceticism to become a morose, anti-social misanthropist. On the other hand, he should be watchful over the motives that lead him to seek the company of others, because it is his intention that determines whether his social life is pleasing or not in the eyes of God.

He must also be careful of his attitude toward others. Although the reference to our Lady at the marriage of Cana is brief, there is, nevertheless, something in her attitude that merits our consideration. She does not give the impression of being a guest, expecting everyone to make great efforts to make her enjoy the feast, nor did she go there to attract attention, or to take over the whole running of the affair. The fact that she was the first to notice that the wine was running out shows that she was quite alert and had her eye on what was going on: this implies attention, observation, that she was interested in what was taking place around her and not thinking of herself. In the final analysis, this is charity, love of our neighbor, which is the opposite of selfishness, and instead of seeking its own satisfaction seeks the satisfaction of others. And that is the way it should be. Whoever lets himself be carried away by impulses in his social relations runs the risk of being imprudent and sinning either through excess or defect; he tends to live for himself and not for others, to be motivated by selfishness rather than charity and love of his neighbor. In order to live perfection in this matter and give glory to God, it is indispensable that we should have a discreetly observant attitude, sometimes being active, always paying attention to little things that give tone to our conversation and our gestures. A minimum of attention, of awareness of how we appear to others, is necessary if we are not to behave solely according to our nature and as pagans.

But we may discover another, more profound, value in our social relations. Christians, by the very fact of being Christians, are not simply men but also members of the Church, which is the Mystical Body of Christ. There is a marvelous dogma, and most consoling, which is the Communion of Saints. Nothing that a Christian does is indifferent, for everything has a repercussion—sometimes more, sometimes less, decisive—in the Mystical Body, so that everything a Christian does affects the whole, and therefore each of the members. If we put a red-hot bar of iron on a table, the table burns. If we throw a block of ice into a container of warm water, the water loses its warmth. By the mere fact that the Blessed Virgin was there, the wedding feast at Cana was changed; that is to say: everything was not the same as if she had not been there. Jesus was there, too, and perhaps since then marriage has been a sacrament.

By the fact that all Christians are members, that is, parts, of the Mystical Body of Christ, they are united together by a mysterious bond. Unfortunately, they do not think about this very often, and possibly that explains the terrible lack of any sense of responsibility in many Christians of today. We should always remember that even relations based on mere human sympathy should be directed toward God, since the qualities which evoke that sympathy are due to God. The fact that God has placed a man in circumstances which bring him in contact with certain people or groups implies that God has reasons for that and intends something to develop from this contact. There is an order in charity, and those closest to us have a right to expect most; and the closest to us are those who are most intimately related to us by virtue of the circumstances God has ordained. Charity obliges each one to be better. The more we are on fire ourselves, the more will we enkindle the same fire in others. The closer and the more united we are to God, the more good will we do to those around us. Thus social relations constitute an immense and permanent field of influence, a means of intense mutual improvement. There is no one so stupid that we cannot learn something from him, and there is no one so poor that he has nothing to give. With a little care for those around us and a little love of God, each one of us can increase the amount of happiness on this earth: sometimes only a smile is needed, or a little interest in others, or a friendly manner. This enormous field of social relations makes it possible for us in a permanent way to exercise our love of God by treating our neighbor as God himself would treat him, as we would treat God if he took the form of our neighbor: to love God in our brothers, that is to say, in God's children.[1]

This is also a magnificent field for doing apostolate. Unfortunately, this word has been used with so little discretion and has become so common that it no longer suggests exactly—neither more nor less than—what it means. Apostolate is an active desire for the spiritual improvement of others. It is the overflow of interior life, for only those who

---

[1] J. Escrivá de Balaguer, *Christ Is Passing By*, 19, 44, 48, and others.

truly love God feel sorry that he is not loved by all; only those who appreciate and love the Blood of Christ suffer to see that Blood spilled for so many in vain. Only those who love God love their neighbors and are tortured to see them unhappy because they too do not possess him. It is this interior life that prompts them to lead others to God, without scheming, prudery, force, or insistence, but with the perseverance, the tenacity, the conscientiousness, and also the gentleness that come from grace, helping them to love God and giving them a new outlook on things. Thus the most ordinary conversation can easily and smoothly lead up to fundamental topics that may guide a soul to God and awaken desires of living close to him.

A Christian's social life, therefore, holds tremendous responsibilities. If a Christian shirks his social duties it may mean that he is abandoning all civil life and its problems to the powers of evil, when in fact he should seek and find his own sanctity precisely in those problems. Let us think of society as an organism whose various functions are fulfilled by certain specific organs. If these organs do not function properly, everything goes badly. Everything we see comes to us through our eyes, so if the eyes are damaged we cannot see. If the organs through which the judicial, educational, administrative, and communicative functions operate are damaged, *nothing* will work properly, with enormously evil consequences to society, and ultimately to the salvation of its members. "All the things of this earth, inclusive of its material creatures and the temporal affairs of men, must be brought back—and after sin, redeemed and reconciled—to God. Each one will follow its own nature in accordance with the immediate end given it by God, but envisioning its ultimate supernatural destiny in Jesus Christ: 'For it has pleased God the Father that in him all his fullness should dwell, and that through him he should reconcile to himself all things, whether on the earth or in the heavens, making peace through the blood of his cross' (Col 1: 19–20). We must place Christ at the apex of all human activities." [2]

---

[2] J. Escrivá de Balaguer, Letter, Rome, March 19, 1954, no 7.

Let us consider for a moment another matter that concerns this paradoxical society which calls itself Christian. Any social atmosphere is created by the relationships between the members of that society. How is it, then, that the social atmosphere created by relations among Christians is, so frequently, completely pagan? We allow ourselves to be carried away by fashions, diversions, social gatherings that are not Christian in spirit but are nevertheless supported and cultivated, and sometimes even financed, by Christians. This enormous lack of personality is the result of a previous lack of spiritual life. In the minds of many Christians the old liberal idea still lingers on: that religion, Christ, should be confined to the Church and the pulpit and have nothing to do with everyday life; that the sacred should be separated from the profane. This is precisely the opposite of the way things should be: Christ should be placed at the center of society, so that his spirit may permeate all human activities, transforming and renewing them. We have within our grasp the means of doing this: our ordinary social life. But we must be deeply rooted in the spirit of Christ, possess a strong moral sense and a solid interior life, we must be like red-hot irons; otherwise, instead of influencing our environment, it is our environment—as so often happens— which will overpower us, change us as it likes, and make us slaves of worldliness. Only those who carry their own atmosphere with them wherever they go and know how to radiate it discreetly, without imposing it by force or argument, can give society a Christian tone; and only those can influence their environment for the good. The first Christians acted in this way, and they were able to change the face of society.

"'Environment is such an influence,' you've told me. And I have had to answer: No doubt. That's why you have to be formed in such a way that you can carry your own environment about with you in a natural manner, and so give your own tone to the society in which you live. And then, when you've acquired this spirit, I'm sure you'll tell me with all the amazement of the early disciples as they contemplated the first fruits of the miracles performed by their hands in Christ's name: 'How great is our influence on our environment!' " [3]

Our Lady's prayer

The *Magnificat* and the brief remark that our Lady made to her Son at Cana on behalf of the newly-married couple are the only examples of her prayer that have been recorded by the evangelists. The *Magnificat* is a prayer of praise, in which Mary's heart overflows with love, with words of thanksgiving, with joyful expressions of admiration at the greatness of the Creator and his creation. At Cana, on the other hand, her prayer was one of petition.

It is a phrase of only a few words: "They have no wine." It is so concise, so brief, that it hardly seems a prayer at all. In its very brevity, however, there is such a depth of unsuspected meaning that it would be well for us to examine it at some length.

The first thing we notice in the petition is its simplicity. It is a statement of a need, made with the naturalness of a child. Children do not really ask for what they need: they just say what they want, and there is no need tThe first thing we notice in nts understand them so well that the most fragmentary phrases are clearer for them than a long explanation. The Virgin was the most perfect of creatures, rather, *the* perfect creature, and therefore her prayer was, without doubt, the most perfect prayer, the most beautiful which possesses all the right qualities in the highest degree. For these good reasons it can be taken as the model for our petitions.[4]

Then we see that every prayer should be simple; that is to say, simplicity is the first condition that makes a prayer pleasing to God. Simple is the opposite of complicated, and everything complicated—which is not the same as complex—has an element of artificiality and affectation which impedes the direct and spontaneous expression of intimate feelings. If a prayer is not simple, extraneous considerations

[3] J. Escrivá de Balaguer, *The Way*, 376.
[4] *Christ Is Passing By*, 174.

and influences come between the soul and God that cloud
the pure relationship between creature and Creator; it is no
longer a cry from the depths of a soul standing naked before
its Maker, and instead it becomes a formal conversation with
great attention to protocol and a careful choice of words and
expressions, between an inferior and a superior. If prayer is
not simple, instead of being a conversation between a Son
and his Father it will be like that between a soldier and his
general, or between a cultured and well-educated lady used
to high society and a host who has invited her to dinner. And
this is not what our Lord wants. Perhaps it was because he
knew how complicated we are that he told us to become like
children (Lk 18: 17); that is why he told us to use few words
when we pray and not to be like the pagans who think that
they will be heard because of the abundance of their words,
for our Father knows our needs before we ask him (Mt 6: 7–
8). Jesus himself gave us a perfect lesson of simplicity in
prayer when he taught us the Our Father. How annoying
and pedantic it would be for a child to make a speech in the
language of Demosthenes or Castelar in order to ask his
parents for a slice of bread; but we are equally ridiculous
when we look for formal and affected phrases when speaking
to God. There is a striking contrast between the prayer of
the Pharisee and that of the publican (Lk 18: 9ff.); in which
we can see that simplicity is always the external expression of
sincerity so deeply and intimately lived that it shows itself
spontaneously even in the most insignificant details of our
everyday life.

The second characteristic of our Lady's prayer is the humility apparent in her request. Grammatically speaking, the
phrase is not a petition at all; but her wish is clear: she was
not simply relating an item of gossip, it is obvious that she
wanted Jesus to remedy the situation. Her humility, however, was such that she did not want to trouble Jesus. He was
her Son, but he was God, as she knew it very well, as she also
very well knew that he was the Messiah, and his mission
came first and nothing else should be allowed to interfere
with it. Her spontaneous statement of the situation, the extreme delicacy with which she approached Jesus, her almost

shy way of hinting rather than requesting, all show a clear awareness of the distance, and at the same time the closeness, between the two of them: he was God, but she was his mother. Only someone as humble as Mary could give precisely this tone and shade to such a prayer, making it so forceful and at the same time asking nothing. It showed a great helplessness, as if suggesting that she would not have troubled him if she could remedy the damage herself; it also showed such anxiety and interest in the situation as if to say that she approached him as the only solution. What appeals most strongly to the mercy of God is not our words but our helplessness; therefore, it is the prayer that comes from our humility and destitution that most strongly "forces" God to help us. What makes us pray most intensely, what makes us put our whole soul into it, is our necessity; and no one but a humble man can realize how gravely he needs God's mercy, how much he depends on God, and how true it is that he can only sow and water, but it is God who gives growth (1 Cor 3:6–7).

We, who are not humble, have not sufficient delicacy to ask God for anything. Very often our selfishness makes us treat him thoughtlessly, as if he were our servant, whose only function was to solve the problems we ourselves create or get us out of trouble caused by our own stupidity. We are not interested in requesting things for others; we seldom forget ourselves and think of those who are in worse need; we frequently confine our petitions to small, purely earthly things, as if our life depended on them, while we easily neglect the only thing that really matters. Sometimes we even try to "bargain" with God: "You do this for me, and I will do that for you; you help me out here, and I promise to do this in return." And perhaps then, when we get what we wanted, we look for a way to avoid what we promised, since it no longer has any use. This bargaining brings our selfishness beyond all limits. The absence of love becomes too blatant. We become odious egotists, thinking solely of our own interests, expecting everyone, even God, to be at our service. Not that is it wrong, of course, to seek remedies for our earthly ills: our Lady's example at Cana shows that. And Jesus himself taught us to ask for our daily bread. But we should not forget that all the other petitions in the Our Father are of a different kind. What is wrong is that we should ask for things as if we deserved them, as if we had some right to them other than God's love and goodness toward us, as if he owed them to us.

Perhaps the thing that is most noteworthy in the Virgin's prayer at Cana is her faith in her Son. She was his mother, she had seen him sleeping in her arms, nevertheless, she did not venture to tell him what he should do. She merely pointed out the problem to him and left the rest to his own judgment, convinced that whatever solution he offered, no matter what he decided, was the best possible; she left the matter entirely to him, leaving him completely free to do his own will without any feeling of obligation. And why? Because she knew that whatever he chose to do would be the most perfect thing that could be done, and the problem would be solved in the best possible way. She did not tie his hands, so to speak, or force him to take one line of action, determining a certain mode of action for him; she trusted in his wisdom, in his superior knowledge, in his wider and deeper vision of things, which took in aspects and circumstances perhaps unknown to her. She did not even ask herself whether he would think fit to intervene or not: she merely pointed out the problem and left it in his hands. The fact is that faith "puts God under an obligation" more than the most skillful and forceful arguments. When the Virgin spoke to him, his hour had not yet come: she spoke to him, and immediately his hour came.[5] As St. John says, this was his first miracle (Jn 2: 11). Mary's faith, contained in these few words, overcame time, hastened the hour when our Lord would manifest his divinity by a miracle.

How differently we ourselves act! When we ask God for something, very rarely do we confine ourselves to showing God our nakedness, our lack of whatever it is we want because it is necessary, useful, or convenient for us. Usually we ask not simply for a solution but for a *particular* solution that

[5] See J. Escrivá de Balaguer, *A Priest Forever*.

we have already thought out. We restrict God's action to only one possible solution, the solution that we, with our tiny intelligence, consider the most fitting. We harass the Lord; we urge him to exert his power in the execution of our designs; we take all initiative from him and show more faith in our capacity to find adequate solutions than in his. We think that if we are not absolutely specific and clear about what we want we run the risk of being overlooked by God and getting the wrong solution. We start off on the presumption that no one, not even God, knows better what we need than we ourselves. And if, by chance, we do not get what we ask for at once, our prayer becomes weaker and weaker; we think that God is not going to do anything about it, and finally we abandon the prayer as a child abandons an old toy of which he is tired. From time to time we should remember the answer that Jesus gave to the mother of James and John when she asked for something absurd: "You do not know what you are asking" (Mt 20:22). There are occasions when our limited intelligence and our blind selfishness make us ask for things that in the final analysis would do us more harm than good, or at least are simply absurd. And there is no natural or supernatural reason that can force God to help us in our mad designs.

It is true that prayer is omnipotent: as St. Augustine says, it is the strength of man and the weakness of God. But this is true only when it is really prayer. To pray is to elevate our hearts to God, not merely to say words. The Jews were not praying properly when God rebuked them through Isaiah: "This people draw near me with their mouth, and with their lips glorify me, but their heart is far from me" (Is 29:13). And by the heart we usually understand "that which is most intimate in us, that which is hidden deepest within us; there where we find only ourselves, exactly as we really are; where we keep all our virtues and defects. . . . The *heart* takes part in everything we thank, say and do. It can either give color and fragrance to it or make it ugly, corrupt and repugnant. The *heart* is in and behind everything that we are and do. It is the very root of our being, the most intimate and hidden nucleus of our person which we ourselves often do not know for that very reason; it is also the standard which God uses to measure up and evaluate everything we do."[6] We pray, then, insofar as we elevate our being toward God, not insofar as we address words to him, for to address words to a person does not always mean that we are turned toward him in mind, projected, as it were, toward him. "For out of the abundance of the heart the mouth speaks" (Mt 12:34). That is why when our Lady's prayer was one of praise a whole torrent of words flowed out in the *Magnificat*, but when her prayer was one of petition she uttered only three or four words. Mary's heart, indeed her whole being, was so completely immersed in God that every word that came from her was laden with dedication to him; and these four words of Cana were an intense prayer because they were spoken from a heart that rested in God. We, on the other hand, with our formal and selfish petitions for trivial and unimportant matters, very often show that although we speak to God with our words, our hearts are turned in upon themselves and not elevated to God, thinking of creatures; our hearts are tied to the things of this world. Prayer is the expression of a loving heart, the breath of the soul; thus, everything that is directed to God is prayer insofar as it is based on simplicity, humility, and faith. That is why there are different degrees of prayer: from the awkward stuttering of someone just beginning to orient his being toward God for the first time to the perfect prayer of the one who has already achieved union with him.

All elevation toward God is prayer; because of this we can always pray, sometimes without even realizing it. And prayer is so important that if it does not exist in some degree and some form—but always from the heart—then there is an end to all interior life, in the same way that our body would die if we stopped breathing. And to elevate our being to God is easy, so easy that anyone can do it. Our Lord has shown us the way: all we have to do is try to be simple, humble, and trusting; God will do the rest, for he is always found by those who seek him with a pure heart.[7]

---

[6] Franz M. Moschner, *Christian Prayer*.
[7] See J. Escrivá de Balaguer, *Friends of God*, 247.

" . . . *Do ye*"

Whatever way we look at it, our Lady does not play a leading part in the Gospel. In the first chapter of St. Luke she plays the important role of protagonist; in the second chapter, although she is still quite important, she is no longer the protagonist: her Son has taken her place. Of her own life and her part in the Gospel she could very appropriately have used St. John the Baptist's phrase: "He must increase; but I must decrease" (Jn 3:30). When our Lord begins his public life she returns to obscurity, and after the feast at Cana she is mentioned only two or three times more, and then very briefly. Even on that last terrible occasion the evangelists give us no idea of the greatness of the Victim's mother; all they say is that she was there.

When St. Luke had to mention her, he let us know exactly what she said. We know her dialogues with the angel Gabriel and with Elizabeth. We also know some of the things that she said to Jesus. But we cannot say that she forgot us, her other children whom she conceived when Christ redeemed us all on the Cross. She does not, it is true, say very much to us: in fact, she says one phrase, but it is very definite and clear and concise.

In the house at Cana where the wedding took place there were a number of men-servants. We know nothing more about them: neither their ages, their faces, their temperaments, their background, how many there were, not even their names. We do not need to know any more; and the only means we have of identifying ourselves in them, precisely, that they are described by those two conditions which we all fulfill: they were human beings, and they were servants. For we all, by the very fact of being creatures, are servants of God in his plan of creation. To us, then, are addressed these clear and precise words: "Do whatever he tells you" (Jn 2:5). Perhaps we are tempted to think that the phrase does not say very much, that it is rather vague and seems to contain no concrete lesson for us. Nevertheless, on this occasion, and with only those few short words, our Lady again gives testimony to her complete perfection: she says no more and no less than is necessary. Here again she strikes the perfect mean; what else could she say to us?

In fact, there was no reason why she should explain anything to us. The message of salvation had been entrusted to her Son; he alone had been sent by the Father to manifest the kingdom of God, to announce the coming glory, to complete the revelation of what still remained hidden. Mary was the Mother of the Messiah; her mission had been clearly defined, and it contained nothing she was meant to communicate to us. Jesus, on the other hand, was the Messenger, and the Father had given testimony of him.

He did not speak in his own name but in the name of the Father who had sent him and ordained what he should say and how he should say it; he was not to modify what the Father had said to him but repeat it as it had been told to him (Jn 12:49–50). He was to say only the things that he had heard from the Father (Jn 8:26). He, in his turn, sent his disciples into the world in the same way that the Father had sent him (Jn 17:18).

The whole Gospel and everything in it, characters and events, revolves around Jesus. He is the center; his mother is not, even though she is so close to him that no other creature, however great and exceptional his sanctity and union with God, will ever equal her. It was precisely because she was so close to her Son that she was able to adjust herself so well to her own position without ever going beyond the proper limits. Only he who is sent can convey a message; it is entrusted to him and no one else; he alone has authority to communicate things because of his character as messenger; but he does not speak for himself or in his own name but in the name of him who sends him. As far as transmission of the Good News was concerned, our Lady, in spite of her important and unique mission, had no part to play. The Father sent his only-begotten Son; he, in his turn, sent his apostles, and they, in turn, sent their disciples and successors. Only the hierarchy of the Church has this character of having been sent. Only the hierarchy is invested with the faculty of teaching on matters concerning the Gospel or questions of faith.

The Blessed Virgin was too discreet and humble to impose on anyone her own opinion or advice, nor had she anything to reveal. Therefore, the only time she ever addressed us, she displayed the same discretion and prudence that she showed in everything else: "Do whatever he tells you." This may seem to mean little to those for whom the Gospel is just a collection of well known and often repeated phrases with no real interest for them; for those who, through lack of meditation, have no understanding of the words of God, and have made it a mere topic of conversation, without ever considering what it really means. In fact, this brief counsel of the Virgin is worth whole volumes.

Our Lady asks us to do, not just something, but precisely what he tells us to do. Before doing it, then, we must listen to God and find out what it is that he wants of us; otherwise we will not know what we are supposed to do. We must listen, not just to *anyone*, but to her Son, the Messenger of the Father, because only he has been sent to speak to us. It would be impossible to listen to him if he had said nothing. But he did speak to us: and besides, he took the trouble of ensuring that the things he said, or at least those of concern to us, should be transmitted, collected, and written down so that, two thousand years later, we should be able to read them and listen to him again.

Here we come across something few people seem to understand: that it is more important for a Christian to read the Gospel than people usually think; it is certainly more important than to read any other book, whatever it may be. We Christians are usually quite convinced that we know Jesus Christ, that we know his teaching and everything that we should know. But we may be greatly deceived if we believe that we know sufficiently, for everyone's knowledge should be in accordance with what he is: a six-year-old child who learns his catechism undoubtedly knows his religion; but an engineer, a doctor, a professor, a writer, or any intellectual thirty or forty years old who knows no more than the catechism has indeed a most impressive ignorance of his religion, even if he hears a sermon at Mass every Sunday. What the Lord says to us is written in the Gospel, and anyone who wishes to know it must read it there, read it frequently, assimilate it by repeated reflection: then he will pay more attention to the Church's ordinary Magisterium and understand its teachings; then the voice of grace will make itself heard in him. We cannot say that a person listens to what Christ says unless he reads the Gospel.

"Do whatever he tells you." The most important thing of all is that we should do it. But our Lady wants us to do *exactly* what he tells us. But doing what someone else tells us to do and not always what we would like to do ourselves is called obedience. What our Lady recommends, then, is that we should obey, that is, put all our personal initiative, not into what we want to do, but what God tells us to do.

This is undoubtedly good advice, for who can be sure of not being led astray by the follies of his own erring mind? Who can think that he is infallible? Jesus, on the other hand, never errs because he is the Truth, and when he speaks he always says what the Father has taught him (Jn 8:28), the truth he heard from God (Jn 8:40), which leads to eternal life (Jn 12:49–50). Good advice, to be sure, but does it not demand too much? Is it not like asking us to give up the two highest and noblest faculties we possess? In asking us to do what he tells us is our Lady not asking us to direct our intelligence to his word, to believe him without question and follow him? Is she not asking as to violate our free will in carrying out his commands?

No one can say that Jesus Christ was not free, completely free. Nevertheless, he spoke only those things he had heard from him who sent him (Jn 8:26); what is more, he was obedient unto death, even to the death of the Cross (Phil 2:8). Therefore there is, there can be, no incompatibility between freedom and obedience, either on the level of the intelligence or of action. So true is this that Christ himself said: "If you continue in my word, you are truly my disciples indeed, and you will know the truth, and the truth will make you free" (Jn 8:31–32). This statement caused a great furor among the Jews who were listening to him, and our Lord went on to explain: "Everyone who commits sin is a slave to sin" (Jn 8:34). The connection between the different truths or, rather, the different aspects that constitute the one, single truth, which is revelation, becomes more evident: humility is truth, truth makes us free, he is free who has no sin, for sin separates us from truth, makes us servants of falsehood and pride.

We already said something of freedom when examining our Lady's reply to the angel's message, but perhaps something more could be said here. We have grown too accustomed to an erroneous idea of freedom as being a power to choose between good and evil, or among several things, some of which are better than others. But this—which happens, of course—is due not to our freedom but to the imperfection of our freedom. If freedom consisted in choosing between good and evil, then neither God nor his Son would be free, because God cannot choose evil. And if, of two good things, God could choose the less good, then he would be imperfect. Freedom is, properly speaking, the ability to choose the best, the capacity to desire the most perfect. Man does not in fact always choose the most perfect precisely because he is man, that is, a creature tainted by original sin who has in himself a certain element of slavery. "Every one who commits sin is a slave to sin"; therefore when man— every man—sinned in Adam, he remained subject to a servitude or slavery from which only his personal effort, collaborating with grace, can free him. Thus can we understand the struggle of man to unite himself with God, and that double law of which St. Paul speaks (Rom 7:15–21), which leads to a conflict in man's interior life. To submit our intelligence to the truth contained in the words of Jesus Christ is, in effect, to free it from error. To subject our will to the fulfillment of his commands is to release our human liberty from the bonds that oppress it. We are free to the exact extent to which we are united to Christ—to Truth—by obedience.

Obedience, then, is a key virtue; if we obey God it is enough; everything else follows as a consequence. Moreover, obedience is nothing more than the fulfilment of the vocation proper to creatures, for every creature has been made to give glory to God: that is what constitutes his whole *raison d'être*, that is the purpose of his life on earth: that and nothing else—not even salvation, which is itself only a consequence. The will of God is the norm to which we must adjust all our conduct. The first sin in the world was disobedience, and as a result of this disobedience came death and the loss of Paradise. It was through obedience, on the other hand, that reparation was made and hope could return to the heart of man, for it was through obedience that Christ saved us. Disobedience is rebellion, which results in death and damnation: obedience is salvation.

Here a point arises that should be clarified before going any further: Christians very often act according to what we might call the "rule of sin." They are Christians who, before doing or omitting something, always ask themselves whether or not it is a sin—usually meaning grievous sin. If it is not, then they feel justified in doing it or omitting it, because they thank it is something they can do. Apart from the fact that this is erroneous reasoning, for a deliberate venial sin is never allowed for any reason whatsoever, the rule itself is false, for we are not meant simply to avoid offending God but to love him and please him. Any obedience confined to avoiding mortal sins runs the risk of becoming disobedience: as if a son told his parents he had decided not to do anything that would make them throw him out of their house, but that otherwise he would not hesitate to displease and upset them. Consciously to adopt such an attitude toward God would lead to grievous violation of the first of the Commandments.

We should learn how to be truly obedient from those silent servants whom Mary told to do whatever Jesus should command. They put themselves at his disposal immediately; when they were told to fill the water-pots, they filled them to the brim; then they returned to tell Jesus that his orders had been carried out; and, at his direction, they took the wine to be tasted by the chief steward. A miracle was performed, and these anonymous servants cooperated in it.

The first requirement for obedience is willingness. Those men put themselves at Christ's disposal without knowing what he was going to say or what he was going to command them to do. They imposed no conditions; they did not try to find out what he was going to command before deciding whether or not they would do it. They were servants, aware of their position as servants and ready to serve. It is necessary to be thus disposed if we understand what he tells us. As Jesus said to the Jews: "Why is it that you cannot understand the language I talk? It is because you have no ear for the message I bring" (Jn 8:43, Knox). It is not enough to read the Gospels out of mere curiosity or in order to increase our religious knowledge; what we want to do is not to *learn*, but to *improve*. We must approach the Gospel, and Christ, determined *beforehand* to do whatever he tells us. Otherwise it will be very difficult to understand what he says, and obedience will be impossible because the heart is closed to the divine suggestions.

The servants also obeyed immediately. Promptness indeed is essential in obedience. To delay doing our duty is a way, the most cunning way, of not doing it at all; it is similar to the passive resistance of the son whose father told him to go into the vineyard to work, and who said: "I go, Sir," but did not (Mt 21:28ff.). The consequences of delay, procrastination, passivity, unwillingness are immeasurable. Things that would be intolerable, for instance, in a factory or any business seem to us perfectly justified, logical, and natural in the service of God; and how sad it is that all the enthusiasm we put into making a success of our human work, which is rewarded in money, is considered unnecessary, and even out of place, in supernatural work, whose reward is glory. Time is a gift too precious to be wasted, for it may happen that when our time is up we will find that our task is only half finished, the divine scales weighed against us, our work insufficient.

The servants obeyed without saying a word: obedience should also be silent. "Yours should be a silent obedience. That tongue!"[8] Protests, signs of unwillingness, criticism muttered inaudibly or merely thought, remarks that sneer at the master and undermine his authority, all these things make a slave of him who has to "obey," for they show he is

[8] *The Way*, no. 627.

obeying only because he is forced. There is no merit in this kind of obedience. None of the servants asked our Lord for an explanation of why he ordered them to fill the jars with water: we must obey not only with our will but also with our intelligence, using it to think of possible ways of doing what we are ordered, and not to examine everything in a critical spirit, which, ultimately is a sign of pride.[9]

The jars were filled *usque ad summum*, up to the brim. No one could ask for more; the servants did a perfect job. We cannot obey by halves, we must always do a complete job. Anything is done only when it is finished; otherwise, it is still in the process of being done. When someone says that something is "practically finished," we should understand that it is not finished at all, something remains to be done. And what our Lord tells us to do is too important to be left half done; it is never something trivial, to be toyed with, but a serious duty whose significance very often we cannot even suspect.

This, then, is the advice—the only advice—that our Lady has left us: that we should do whatever her Son tells us, obey him willingly, ready to do anything; that we should obey promptly, silently, fully, not only with our will but also with our intelligence, with our heart, putting our whole being into it; as she did, as he did.

---

[9] *Christ Is Passing By*, no. 42.

6

MOTHER OF SORROWS

> But standing by the cross of Jesus were his mother and his mother's sister, Mary, the wife of Clopas, and Mary Magdalene. When Jesus saw his mother, and the disciple whom he loved standing near, he said to his mother, "Woman, behold your son!" Then he said to the disciple, "Behold, your mother!" And from that hour the disciple took her to his own home.
>
> JOHN 19:25–27

At the foot of the cross

As Giuseppe Ricciotti remarked in *The Life of Christ*, in the Gospels there is no note of joy when Jesus is born and no expression of sorrow when he dies. It is indeed characteristic of the Gospels to show such sobriety, which excludes all intentional lyricism, all elaboration, all commentaries, all argument. With exemplary objectivity the Gospels simply record facts, statements, truths, events, with no attempt at method, with the spontaneity and richness of life itself. None of the evangelists intended to write history; they wrote only to teach, to give testimony of the truth they had seen and heard. Everything is centered on the Person and the message of Jesus. At that culminating moment, the sacrifice of the Son of God on the Cross, our attention is concentrated on him to such an extent that the Passion constitutes a unity in itself, systematically compact and indivisible. The Cross is the point of convergence of Jesus' entire life; it is the goal toward which every one of his actions was directed from the very moment of the Incarnation; it is the center, the consummation of the mission with which the Father had entrusted him. "At the sight of Christ bruised and broken—

just a lifeless body taken down from the cross and given to his Mother—at the sight of Jesus destroyed in this way, we might have thought he had failed utterly. Where are the crowds that once followed him, where is the kingdom he foretold? But this is victory, not defeat. We are nearer the Resurrection than ever before; we are going to see the triumph which he has won with his obedience." [1]

From a purely human point of view, the Crucifixion, the end of Christ's life on earth, is without doubt the greatest of all failures: a disgraceful and shameful death on the Cross, accompanied by two convicted criminals, after being judged by the religious leaders of his own people and condemned with the consent of the representative of Roman authority; accompanied in his agony by the sarcasm and contempt of those who accused him of being an imposter and possessed by the devil. And his Mother was there, looking at him, seeing everything, hearing all the scorn and derision, letting the pain, the humiliation, and the desolation of her Son penetrate her soul as intimately as had grace at the moment of the Incarnation. No human being ever suffered any agony that could even be compared with Mary's. For her, too, it was a culminating moment, as decisive as that in which the angel appeared to her and asked for her decision. And in the same way as her life previous to the Annunciation had prepared her for the angel's visit, so too God had prepared her for this supreme hour. The sword foretold by Simeon long ago, when Mary held the little Child in her arms, was now a bloody reality. The evangelists do not tell us how Mary spent the time from the beginning of the Last Supper to the terrible drama of Golgotha. It has been said that she received private revelations: this is quite possible, but we do not know whether it is true. She was with the women and perhaps with that intuition which all mothers have in things concerning their children, she had some presentiment of the terrible things that were about to happen. We cannot, however, presume any of these things without running the risk of being carried away by our imagination, solving too simply a

[1] J. Escrivá de Balaguer, *Christ Is Passing By*, 95.

question that requires study and understanding, separating the Blessed Virgin too much from ourselves, by placing her on a magical and fantastic level, as the apocryphal gospels treat the flight into Egypt and the infancy of Jesus. The Venerable Anne Catherine Eymerich had several visions of the Passion, all set down in a book that gives an almost minute by minute account of what our Lady did and thought during those bitter hours. The most demanding imagination will find there a full answer to all possible questions, and even the most curious will be satisfied.

What we gather from the Gospel is that our Lady did not receive any sudden enlightenment as to the Redemption and how it was to be achieved. Otherwise, St. Luke would not have said that "they did not understand the saying which he spoke to them" when Mary and Joseph found the Child Jesus in the Temple: if she had known everything beforehand she would have completely understood Jesus' answer and all its implications. We have no reason to except our Lady from the law of gradual growth to which the son of God himself was subject: growth in wisdom, in understanding and penetration of the mysteries, of the mystery of her Son, above all.

Simeon's distressing prophecy, the Child's incomprehensible answer in the Temple after the anguish his absence had caused, the apparent indifference with which Jesus treated her when she went with his "brethren" to meet him (Mt 12:46ff.), the pondering in her heart of that mysterious and terrible passage of Isaiah about the "man of sorrows," Jesus' gradual separation from her when he left Nazareth and gave himself up completely to his mission, her knowledge of the announcement of his Passion, which Jesus made to his disciples—all these things were so many insinuations by which God slowly prepared her for the great moment of the Redemption. The Virgin observed the gradual change that was taking place in the people's attitude to her Son: from the great enthusiasm caused by his miracles and his words to the terrible solitude of the last months, when nobody dared to be favorable to him for fear of being expelled from the synagogue. She saw how great clouds were gathering over Jesus, darkening the bright atmosphere that had surrounded the beginning of his public life; she heard the rumors that the Pharisees were accusing him of being possessed by the devil; and she saw how even his friends did not believe in him. If the disciples could feel a chill in the atmosphere and sometimes had to go with the Master far from Jerusalem because the Jews were going to kill him, we can be certain that this could not escape Mary's penetration and intuition, with her habitual meditation on everything she observed. When the hour came, the disciples fled, but Mary remained at the foot of the Cross near her Son; she was prepared, she was ready for anything, even this.

The *stabat* of which St. John speaks is a very definite point of reference. So also is the old and venerable tradition of the meeting between Mother and Son when he was on his way to Calvary, dirty and ragged, carrying on his bleeding shoulders the wood to which he was to be nailed. She saw everything that we know to have happened on Calvary, and many things that are unrecorded. Willam makes a remark about Mary's unique disposition of soul that is especially relevant here. Any mother, at the death of her child, can easily recall his entire life, and especially the events directly leading up to his death. The Virgin was accustomed to meditation, to thinking about things, relating them to one another and discovering their interior unity; and she always remembered back to the starting point, to the moment when the angel revealed to her the magnificence of God's plan: "If we keep this in mind we can see how, for Mary, standing at the foot of the Cross, the entire life of her Son lived again in her memory." She had many motives, indeed, for remembering his life. It was as if God wished to manifest the intimate connection between the drama on Calvary and the joyful period that began with the Annunciation.

From where she stood she could read the inscription over his head: *Jesus Nazarenus, Rex Judeorum*. "Thou shalt call his name Jesus," the angel had said; the prophets had called him "the Nazarene"; and Gabriel had added: "The Lord God shall give unto him the throne of David his father: and he shall reign in the house of Jacob for ever. And of his kingdom there shall be no end." All that seemed like a cruel mockery of anyone who might, quite logically, picture to himself the splendor of a real throne and the grandeur of a real savior: the throne was the cross of a condemned criminal, guarded by jeering soldiers, and the Savior could not save himself. She could not help but hear these things from the filthy mouths of those who stood around the Cross, curious to see the proceedings, enjoying their triumph, and smiling sardonically ". . . the chief priests, with the scribes and elders, mocked him, saying, "He saved others; he cannot save himself. He is the king of Israel; let him come down now from the cross, and we will believe in him. He trusts in God; let God deliver him now, if he desires him; for he said, 'I am the Son of God' " (Mt 27:41–43). And once again she thought of those words which she could never forget, which she had repeated and pondered so often: ". . . the child to be born will be called holy, the Son of God" (Lk 1:35). Everything the angel had told her about Christ's destiny was being fulfilled, but in a completely different way from what might humanly be expected.

This violent contrast between the hope and its accomplishment, the promises fulfilled in a manner that, to faithless eyes, would have seemed a tragic jest of fate, the *stabat* of the mother tasting drop by drop the chalice of a never-equalled sorrow, would have been an ideal subject for an ancient Greek tragedy. Sorrow would have been immortalized in the mother, standing beside her dying Son bleeding in agony on the cross, dark clouds gathering around her, with no hope of consolation, and humiliated by the sarcasm and contempt of her enemies celebrating their triumph. But no Greek tragedy was written, there was no declamation, no chorus: nothing but the dry, brief words of a few men who gave testimony of what happened. Before Christ there was tragedy because Destiny ruled; after Christ tragedy is impossible, because he has revealed to us the will of the Father. Tragedy is possible only where faith in a paternal God is supplanted by the sense of an implacable fatalism that man is abandoned to the caprices of a cruel fate, indifferent to human sufferings. All the hardness and cruelty usually associated with the word "Destiny" come precisely from its dissociation from faith in God, because Destiny is the pagan term for God's plan and is the consequence of man's rebellion against the divine will. Romano Guardini mentions some of the most characteristic points with masterly precision: "When I pronounce the word 'destiny' I feel that what it signifies is very close to me and yet comes from far away. It belongs to me, it is intimately mine, but at the same time it is completely alien to me. . . . It is addressed to me alone, its roots are somewhere else far away; it is, fundamentally, the whole of existence. It is extremely personal; in it I find myself completely alone, isolated, irreplaceable, indestructible and at the same time it links me with everything else. Destiny, according to our experience, is immutable, inevitable and overwhelming. Destiny comes to me from outside myself, but at the same time it is already inside me, within myself. It is not as if I were waiting for the course of time and nature to bring my destiny to me, but rather I myself am my own destiny. Finally, I experience my destiny as something rather divine. It is filled with mysterious energy and has power over me. . . . In all things, a will, which is not mine, makes itself manifest, causing them to happen the way they do, and keeping them in existence, without ever even letting me know why; however much my will rebels against them."

Ancient paganism, indeed all paganism, when it attempted to probe the mystery of existence, found itself confronted with the insecurity of the unknown. Christ is the light, and with him *knowledge* came to us. Knowledge is what gives man security; it frees him from anguish and terror. The unknown—not necessarily the mysterious—the dark forces that rise up within him from without, threaten the order of his life by launching him into the unexpected and the unforeseen; all paralyze his faculties; they confront him with something of which he has no knowledge but which is completely alien to himself. Anxiety, terror, that unbearable fear of something that takes a hold on life and oppresses it, all disappear in the saints and give way to an attitude of mastery toward the world, of imperturbable security in the face of any event, of understanding everything because everything means something to them and they know where it comes from and where it leads. Living close to God through grace gives a full understanding of how everything in the universe has its place in God's plan; and this knowledge is the foundation of their serene attitude to life and everything life may bring. Pain, illness, suffering, the greatest catastrophes, are not blind forces unloosed on the world by chance; rather, they are obedient creatures fulfilling their own part in the universe, conducing to the salvation of God's elect.

One cannot speak of the *tragedy* of Calvary because there can be no tragedy in relation to Jesus or Mary. The fulfillment of God's will can never be tragic. Tragedy supposes a blind and cruel fate that preys on man and oppresses him, which never understands him and is indifferent to his suffering. A Christian, therefore, can never feel that he is a victim of fate provided he is genuinely Christian; that is, for him there is no such thing as Destiny; if he is united to Christ and participates in his life, then he is not the object of blind Destiny but of intelligent Design; there can be no blind fate, but God's loving and paternal care. On the other hand, when man cuts himself off from Christ, when he rejects the light, then he remains blind and gropes in darkness, he understands nothing, he finds himself whirled about by unknown forces in the face of which he does not know what to do, he is left a prisoner of his own helplessness; then, indeed, he creates his own tragedy. Since Christ, a tragic fate is possible only for those who choose it by rebelling against God.

No one can suggest that God did not love the Blessed Virgin. Nevertheless, he did not exempt her from Calvary or from making her participate in the Cross to a fuller extent than anyone else in the world except her Son. It would be foolish—in a Christian, unpardonably foolish—to think that if God really loves us, as he does, he will exempt us from the Cross, the sign of the Christian. It would be well to recall those clear and vigorous passages in St. Paul in which he teaches us the importance that the Cross has in the life of a disciple of Christ; it would be especially well to remember the Cross nowadays, when the sense of the supernatural is darkened and many try to live a too natural, too human

Christianity, adapted to the world and their own comfort. As St. Paul wrote, "For the word of the cross is folly to those who are perishing, but to us who are being saved it is the power of God" (1 Cor 1: 18). In another place he wrote: "For many, of whom I have often told you and now tell you even with tears, live as enemies of the cross of Christ. Their end is destruction, their god is the belly, and they glory in their shame, with minds set on earthly things" (Phil 3: 18–19).

There are indeed many—including Christians—who act as if they were enemies of the Cross of Christ, many for whom the preaching of the Cross seems foolishness; many who flee from the Cross as from the devil; for whom the word "mortification" is unintelligible; for whom penance is something that belongs to the narrow and superstitious mentality of the past. These people generally have suffocated their sense of sin and responsibility, if they have not lost it altogether; they are monumentally ignorant of Christianity itself: they lack any brotherhood whatsoever with Christ, the "first of the brethren," the head of the Body to which, as Christians, they belong.

The Virgin could have taken refuge in the sympathetic company of the women, in the intimacy of her home, far away from Calvary; after all, there was nothing she could do, and her presence neither avoided nor relieved the sufferings and humiliation of her Son. But she was there, nevertheless. But she did not stay with Christ for the same reason as any mother stays beside the deathbed of her son instead of going out to try to enjoy herself when she sees that she can neither keep him alive nor stop his suffering. No, the Virgin Mary identified herself with her Son; her love made her suffer with him since there was nothing else she could do. Because she loved him and because love unites, she suffered with him; her love could not stand separation, not even in that terrible moment; she preferred suffering, however great it might be.

There is a precise and very direct relationship between the capacity to love and the capacity to suffer. He who is not capable of suffering is incapable of loving. The reason the saints have so eagerly embraced suffering is that their love for Christ led them to suffer with him. The fact that we do not embrace suffering but, on the contrary, avoid it is a sign that we still love ourselves too much. Every now and then we should examine our love of the Cross in order to estimate our love of God: we love God to the same extent that we love the Cross. The Cross is the only way of uniting earth with heaven: if we reject it we reject the means of our salvation. Thus, faithfulness to Christ on Calvary, acceptance of the Cross, is both a sign that we are on the path to salvation, and a proof of love on the part of God.

The sacrifice of her Son

The Fathers of the Church and later theologians have always interpreted St. John's account of the Blessed Virgin standing at the foot of the Cross as something more than merely watching what was happening. In order to present her simply as an onlooker, the evangelist would have said *erat*. *Stare*, to stand, would indicate that he wants to stress the fact of the Virgin's standing, and we know how meaningful this act is in the symbolism of the Church's liturgy. When, for instance, the faithful stand up for the reading of the Gospel at Mass, it is an external expression of an inner attitude of soul, a disposition of acceptance of everything the Gospel teaches, an active and resolute adherence to the message, their identification with it. Mary stood at the foot of the Cross of her Son participating actively and intimately in the sacrifice, identifying herself completely with him, agreeing *willingly*, like Jesus, to the fulfillment of the will of the Father.

Now God at last revealed to her all his plan for the restoration of the order of grace which had been violently disrupted by the sin of Adam, and he found her soul completely disposed to prolong the *fiat* that she had spoken many years before when she did not fully know the greatness of the sacrifice that was to be asked of her. Perhaps at that moment on Calvary Mary gave the supreme proof of her faith. A long time previously, when God wished to raise up a people to himself, to live among them and make the Savior spring from among them, he chose one man and tested his faith and firmness, because he needed an exceptional instrument. He commanded Abraham to sacrifice his only son, the son of the promise. Abraham obeyed, but an angel stopped his arm at the moment he was about to strike. Now, at this other moment, the fulfillment of the promise, God needed another instrument of very superior quality, just as the moment itself was very superior. It was she, the blessed among women, the one who was full of grace, who now offered her Son; but this time no one stopped the blow; Mary drank the chalice to the dregs, and she saw before her eyes the life of her Son, whom she had carried in her womb, completely extinguished.

It is not very common to mention temptation when writing of our Lady, nor do Christians usually think of temptation in reference to her. It is clear that since she was born without original sin she was free of all concupiscence and temptations derived from it. But she must have had temptations of another kind, temptations in the sense of trials, just as Jesus had in the desert, for instance; we know, too, that the thought of his Passion caused him anguish and fear, that his soul was filled with sadness and darkness and that he felt terrible depression, which made him pray to his Father in these trembling words: "My Father, if it be possible, let this cup pass from me; nevertheless, not as I will, but as thou wilt" (Mt 26: 39).

During those three hours on Calvary, Mary was weighed down under a trial so terrible that we will never fully understand it and never be able to describe it. She saw them stripping Jesus of his clothes—disrespectful, humiliating; she saw him deserted by those who had once acclaimed him, by those for whom he had worked miracles, by his disciples, who were now ashamed of him. She saw the chief priests of her people, the highest authorities of the Temple, insulting him, challenging him to come down from the Cross as a proof of his divinity. She saw how Jesus kept silent, how he did not defend himself from accusations levied against him, how he did not give them the proof they demanded: it was as if his power had vanished the moment he fell into the hands of his enemies; as if they were right all along. She knew that her Son was innocent, that he was the Son of God, that he had done only good to others and had never hurt anyone. And God raised not a finger to defend his Son, as if he did not care.

The trial reached its crisis with that cry from Jesus: "My God, my God, why hast thou forsaken me? " (Mk 15:34). It is the moment of greatest desolation, the hour of greatest darkness; the breakdown of everything human, as if Jesus had lost all the courage he had had from knowing he was sustained by his Father. Mary had heard Jesus asking the Father to forgive those who were crucifying him because they knew not what they were doing. She had heard him promise Paradise to one of the thieves beside him. Between Father and Son there was perfect communication; and then suddenly the horrible thing happened; it seemed as if Jesus now found nothing, a blank, where before he had found the Father. Before: "This is my beloved Son . . ." and now: "My God, why hast thou forsaken me? " . . . Mary's hideous temptation, the temptation of abandoning the Father for the Son.

But again our Lady rose to the heights God expected of her. She loved her Son as no other mother is capable of loving. But she did not love Jesus at the expense of, or above the will of, the Father. On the contrary, she loved and accepted the will of the Father even at the cost of her Son and above him, if we may use these expressions. And this does not mean that she had no feelings, or was hard-hearted or insensitive. Rather, she had to have a big courageous heart to bear all this pain without shirking.

Our Lady did not merely stand and watch the drama taking place, helpless to prevent or change it. Her participation was active; she was no mere spectator. She consented to it all. She did not intercede for her Son: she did not beg for mercy or appeal to any friend; she made no effort to change the course of events or in any way to interfere with the will of the Father: she accepted it with respect and left to him all initiative, as at the Annunciation, as always. The Redemption was a great symphony of delivery, of giving Jesus: the Jews, his own people, delivered him to the Gentiles; the

Gentiles delivered him to death; Mary gave him to the will of the Father; Jesus gave himself. It was all done freely, with full consciousness of the deed, in a fully responsible way. This action of our Lady was of such importance that the Church calls her Co-Redemptrix. Her participation was more than mere external assent. It was she who, from her own flesh, gave Jesus the body that was to bear all the suffering. The blood that flowed on the Cross was the same as that which flowed in her veins. It was she who had given him the life that left him through his open wounds. But there was something more important than this. Jesus Christ was God, and he was Life (Jn 14:6), and from this life his mother lived. Mary gave Jesus the life of flesh, and he gave her the life of grace. The bond between them was double; the intimacy between them was singular, exceptional, unique. A Christian is united to the Life of Christ, through grace, by being a member of the Mystical Body; he is part of the entire Christ. The closeness of all the saints to Jesus in his Passion has in all cases been directly related to their degree of sanctity, and to the degree in which they possessed this divine life. The more identified they were with Christ, the more Christ lived in them, the greater was the intensity with which they could feel and participate in his Passion. But Mary was full of grace; she participated in the divine life to the highest possible degree; her union with the Holy Spirit, her Spouse, could not have been more intimate and close. And she was the Mother of the Word made flesh. The union between Jesus and Mary was such that Simeon's prophecy was no mere metaphor.

It is really remarkable what our Lady's faith enabled her to do. Her faith in the mystery of Christ kept her constantly by his side right up to the last moment and put mankind on a completely new level. The demands made on Mary's faith can be gathered from these lines, which show the immense gulf the creature full of grace had to bridge in order to remain united with God, the infinite: "Mary believed blindly. Again and again she had to confirm that belief, and each time with more difficulty. Her faith was greater, more heroic than that of any other human being. Involuntarily we call to mind Abraham and the sudden, terrible sublimity of his faith; but more was demanded of Mary than Abraham. For years she had to combat an only too natural confusion. Who was this 'Holy One' whom she, a mere girl, had borne? This 'great' one she had suckled and known in all his helplessness? Later she had to struggle against the pain of seeing him steadily outgrow her love, even purposely flee it to that realm of ineffable remoteness which she could not enter. Not only did she have to accept this, but to rejoice in it as in the fulfillment of God's will. Not understanding, never was she to lose heart, never to fall behind. Inwardly she accompanied the incomprehensible figure of her Son every step of his journey, however dark. Perseverance in faith even on Calvary—this was Mary's inimitable greatness.

"And literally, every step the Lord took toward fulfillment of his godly destiny, Mary followed—in bare faith. Comprehension came only with Pentecost. Then she understood all that she had so long reverently stored in her heart." [2]

When our Lord, at the final moment of his life, severed the last link that bound him to the earth, gave her to John, seemed to have forgotten her, and remained there above, raised up on the Cross, between God and men as a mediator and a Way, then again our Lady assented, fully accepting her vocation. She was with him again in his *Consummatum est.* She too, like Christ, accomplished everything to the end.

We were all represented in the Redemption. Furthermore, it was we, by our sins, especially by our rebellion in Adam, who crucified our Lord and pierced the heart of the Virgin with a sword. It was the frenzied clamor of our rebellion that shouted with the Jews: "Crucify him!" It was our cowardice in the face of temptation and our love of comfort that gave Jesus over to the mob to be crucified. But there was one human being who did not stain her hands with blood, who really desired the Redemption, one creature who suffered with the Victim, identified with his intention of reparation and expiation. If our Lord had any consolation in the midst of his desolation, when he was abandoned by every-

[2] Romano Guardini, *The Lord*, I.

one, it was to see that he was supported by Mary; it was the knowledge that his apparent failure was understood and shared by one creature. All that desire of purification felt by humanity, weighed down by sin, sometimes felt only vaguely or in some hidden corner—the most noble—of one's being, was felt by Mary as she offered to God the sacrifice that once and for all paid the debt incurred by Adam.

Sin was necessary for Redemption. Without sin—St. Francis de Sales shared this opinion—the Word would have become flesh in order that the Father could be properly and infinitely adored, but there would have been no Redemption. And we, sinners who crucified the Son of God, still treat sin lightly. We think too little and too superficially to realize the malice of sin, its tremendous monstrosity, its satanic cruelty. We fail to understand the catastrophe it brings about in creation. It is most sad and depressing to see that there are Christians who pass from the state of grace to the state of sin without the slightest discomfort—their lives carry on as smoothly as if nothing had happened; it is so sad to see that there are Christians living in a habitual state of damnation, of enmity with Christ, of hatred, and not being in the least concerned about it, even taking pleasure in it; Christians without sorrow who, when they go to confession, scarcely feel repentant for having hurt the Innocent Victim, who measure their love for God by the fear that they feel when they think of hell; Christians who completely miss the point of the Passion, who live without being in the least worried by their collaboration in the death of the Lord, who remain cold and indifferent to the sorrow of our Lady. And the Mother of Sorrows is "a Mother with two sons, face to face: him . . . and you."[3] We are the cause of her sorrows.

Our Lady's attitude to sin and sinners is also noteworthy. As the parish priest of Torcy explains to the young village curate; "The Virgin is Innocence. Think what we, the human race, are for her. She, of her nature, hates sin, but she has no experience of it, an experience which even the holiest of saints have never lacked, even St. Francis of Assisi himself,

[3] J. Escrivá de Balaguer, *The Way*, no. 506.

seraphic and all as he was. Only the Virgin's glance is truly child-like, the only child-like glance that has ever deigned to rest on our shame and disgrace. Yes, my son . . . to pray to her well we must feel that glance of hers upon us, not an indulgent glance—for indulgence is always, without exception, accompanied by some bitter experience—but a glance of tender compassion, of sad surprise, of unfathomable sentiments; an inconceivable look, inexpressible, which makes her younger than sin, younger than the race from which she sprang, and though a mother, by grace, Mother of all grace, our little youngest sister." [4]

The fact that she was innocent makes no difference. Pain is not visited only on those who sin. The innocent suffer also, because we are all members of the Mystical Body of Christ. It was Christ, the Head, who suffered most, and after him, his Mother, the most holy of creatures, the closest to Jesus. Well may the Church ascribe to Mary that exclamation: "O all ye that pass by the way, attend, and see if there be any sorrow like to my sorrow."

"Woman, behold thy son"

It was perhaps the last time that Jesus cast his eyes upon his Mother, a glance perhaps as full of feeling as her own when she met him on his way to Calvary. With parched lips and fever-bright eyes, Jesus looked on that courageous and singular woman and said to her, referring to the disciple whom he loved: "Woman, behold thy son." Then looking at John he continued, "Behold thy mother."

Here then is the outline of a great mystery that St. Paul was later to develop with great clarity. The *Ecce filius tuus* expresses the fullness of the Virgin's vocation as a mother; it is the expression of the final consequence of the mystery announced by Gabriel. It was revealed to her at that moment because our Lord was about to die; while he was alive no one could take his place with his disciples, but now he was going to leave them. Besides, her *fiat* had now reached its highest

---

[4] Georges Bernanos, *The Diary of a Country Priest.*

point, she had participated in the Redemption, her faithfulness had passed the final test. Since she had been so closely associated with the Passion and death of her Son; since she was the Co-Redemptrix—as Pope Pius XII says in *Munificentissimus Deus*: "From all eternity it had been decreed that her destiny was to be mysteriously united with Jesus"—hers was the extremely important task of applying the fruits of the Redemption.

It is impossible for us to perceive fully what Mary's innermost reactions must have been. She must have seen in Jesus' words a last gesture of love and solicitude when he entrusted her to the care of the disciple whom he loved best. John must also have appreciated the confidence that our Lord was placing in him in asking him to take care of the one who had given him birth. The Church however, aided by the Holy Spirit, has been able to penetrate this act completely, and has seen poor and helpless humanity, until then the sad offspring of Eve, being born anew with Mary's sorrow on Calvary. The angel Gabriel's revelation to her and the revelation of Jesus mingle together, and constitute one single vocation. For Mary conceived and gave birth to Jesus, but Jesus is the head of the Mystical Body of Christ, which was born of Mary by the death of her Son.

Parallels are often drawn between Eve and Mary, the new Eve; between Adam and Jesus, the new Adam. God's plan of salvation, magnificent in its simplicity, is unfathomable in all its depth, but the more the mind seeks to comprehend it, the more related and unified everything becomes. This is precisely the object of theology: to discover, by means of study informed by faith and under the Magisterium of the Church, the connections between the truths contained in the Redemption. Thus, the relationship between the Redemption and the Fall becomes more and more clear. Likewise, our Lady's function as mother of the redeemed becomes more and more evident. When Jesus said to her *Ecce filius tuus*, he was showing her exactly how she was to continue the mission entrusted to her by God through the angel Gabriel. Her entire life, all her activity, had been directed toward her motherhood of Jesus, and it was not to close with his death. Christ was perpetuated in his Church, he continued to live in those he had redeemed, and that newly-born Church needed maternal care that only she could give. To her care Christ entrusted the first of the redeemed, the disciples. And Mary continued to play her part, without interruption.

After Jesus' burial, the disciples were dejected and confused. They were discouraged and depressed, as if all their hopes and dreams had died with Jesus. They were so downcast that some—those who went to Emmaus—deserted. They thought back on those three years of following Jesus. What a magnificent adventure it had been: they had surrendered themselves completely, leaving home and family and profession, trusting completely in Jesus' word. And now after all that, they found themselves abandoned and disillusioned, with the additional risk of being persecuted for having been foolish enough to follow Jesus. During those hours after Christ's death, Mary's faith was the only bridge in the world abandoned by Jesus that joined the Passion with the Resurrection. The disciples gathered about her, and she began to be their mother, teaching them to wait patiently and serenely, trusting in the promise. For a mother's task is not merely to give birth but to protect, to watch over, to feed, and to rear the new being until he is able to get along on his own. Perhaps the disciples did not even notice that Mary was watching over them, which is not surprising. The author of *The Crowds of Lourdes*, J. K. Huysmans, who had good reason to know, said: "She soothes us and places us in the hands of her Son; but her hands are so light, so delicate, so soft, that the soul touched by them feels nothing."

We do not know how long the Virgin remained on this earth after the Ascension. She looked after the newly-born Church but, as always, discreetly remaining in the background. She was with the disciples when the Holy Spirit descended on them, and perhaps it was not long afterward that she was carried by the angels to a place in Heaven beside her Son. In any case, St. Luke must have known her and learned from her the details of the Annunciation and Jesus' early years.

With the peace and happiness of one who has fulfilled to the very end everything demanded of her, with a deep but tranquil desire to see her Son again, with the hope and joy of one whose goal is within reach: the Virgin Mary must scarcely have noticed the passage of time. More contemplative than ever, she smiled in her heart as she saw the enthusiasm and fervor of those who were being converted to belief in the Lord Jesus. And she who had witnessed the horror of Calvary, the hour of the powers of darkness, had the consolation of seeing death change to life and darkness give way to light.

* * *

On Calvary, beside the Cross, thirty-three years after the Annunciation, the Virgin discovered that God's plan for her encompassed depths that she could never have imagined. From her immediate acceptance of the new, supernatural motherhood which the Lord revealed to her, we can learn an important lesson: it is that we should not be surprised to discover ever new and greater perspectives in our own particular vocation. The Annunciation was not an end, but rather a beginning. Everything preceding it was no more than a preparation for it. The Annunciation—and the revelation of our own vocation—is the real beginning. The Blessed Virgin's life was the realization of her vocation on earth, the development, as it were, of a seed that contained a world of consequences, each one of which required in due course a new and proper response.

Every vocation should develop until it reaches complete fulfilment. It is not sufficient to play our part in its general outlines; each little detail must be carefully accomplished. No ends should be left loose. Only at the moment of our death can we say: *Consummatum est*. Nobody can ever say "I've done my part," and then sit back in self-complacency and comfort. The Annunciation was a joyful mystery for our Lady, "good news of a great joy which will come to all the people" (Lk 2: 10), but it contained mysteries of sorrow and glory. Nothing was demanded of the Blessed Virgin that was outside or above her vocation; everything that happened to her was contained in it. She stood *dolorosa iuxta crucem lacrimosa, dum pendebat filius*: she saw her beloved Son dying in complete desolation as he gave up his spirit (as the Church commemorates on the feast of the Seven Dolors), and all that, as well as her new, spiritual motherhood, was a consequence of her acceptance: her *fiat* included it all.

No one can calculate in advance how much or what his vocation will demand of him. No one *should* stop to calculate. On the contrary, one should always be ready to give more, to discover greater implications, to expect new demands, and never be surprised to find new and wider perspectives.

The Virgin lived to see the first fruits of the Redemption: she had a mission to fulfill regarding them. That was the important thing: the mission, not the consolation. The last things that Christ saw before his death were his own ruin, his mother's sorrow, his one surviving disciple, the triumph of his enemies. Consolation is something accidental, faithfulness is essential. And it is our faithfulness to the mission entrusted to us, to our particular vocation whose importance in the plan of salvation only God knows, that earns us that new name which will be given to each one of us if we triumph: a name "which no one knows except him who receives it" (Rev 2:17), a name that is unique and personal because our mission also is unique and personal.

Our hope, cause of our joy

"When he prepared the heavens, I was present; when with a certain law and compass he enclosed the depths; when he established the sky above, and poised the fountains of waters: when he compassed the sea with its bounds, and set a law to the waters that they should not pass their limits; when he balanced the foundations of the earth: I was with him forming all things, and was delighted every day, playing before him at all times; playing in the world, and my delights were to be with the children of men. Now therefore, ye children, hear me; Blessed are they that keep my ways. Hear instruction and be wise, and refuse it not. Blessed is the man that heareth me, and that watcheth daily at my gates, and waiteth at the posts of my doors. He that shall find me shall find life, and shall have salvation from the Lord" (Prov 8: 27–35).

The Church applies these words of the Book of Proverbs to our Lady. There is no hyperbole or exaggeration in them because, as Hugh of St. Victor says, anything laudatory or gracious in Holy Scripture or in creatures can be used to praise Mary. But even apart from that, the passage quoted has a more particular application. "He that shall find me shall find life, and shall have salvation from the Lord." Grace is eternal life already begun, and the Virgin possessed it in all its fullness because she was full of grace. To find her is to find life, the life of grace, the Life that she carried in her womb.

When the Church teaches us that devotion to our Lady is a sign and assurance of salvation, she does not say so lightly or merely as a stimulus for pious meditation. The more we think of the doctrine of the Mediation of Mary, the more we appreciate the foundation we have for our devotion to her. St. Bernard long ago said that "God willed that we should have nothing which does not pass through the hands of Mary," and Leo XIII, taking up the doctrine of St. Bernardine of Siena, points out in his encyclical *Fucundi Semper* that "every grace that this world receives is ordinarily distributed in three steps: from God to Christ, from Christ to the Virgin, and from the Virgin to us."

This is easy to understand. Our Lady is our mother, and it is impossible for her to forget her children. It is now her province to exercise the same function in respect of each one of us, the redeemed, as she did for the early Church, and she will always exercise that function: of caring and watching over us. She gives us birth in Christ, she watches over our spiritual growth, she gives us graces we never even suspected we lacked, she removes obstacles from our path, she helps us to get up when we fall. Jesus is the Way to the Father; the Virgin is the straightest, shortest, surest, and easiest way to the Lord, for "To Jesus we always go, and to him we always return, through Mary." ⁵ The power of our heavenly Mother is enormous: How well we know the amazing power of a mother: "Before, by yourself, you couldn't. Now, you've turned to our Lady, and with her, how easy." ⁶ We will always be children in the eyes of the Virgin. It is very difficult to feel grown-up in front of her, because mothers always look on their children as small and helpless. As a mother holds her child, without his noticing it, when he is learning to walk, the Blessed Virgin helps us forward, for she knows how dangerous it is to leave us alone. And even when we rebel and let go her hand and refuse her help, still she does not desert us; she pities us, and her pity is another way of begging her Son to give us grace. Mothers always have a certain weak spot for their delicate, most incapable, and unattractive children: these need their mothers more than the others, even if they do not know it. If the Church calls the Virgin Advocate and Refuge of sinners, it is because time and time again she has shown her particular love for those who need her most, those who would be lost without her.

There are moments in the life of every man when, however much a man he may be, he needs to become a child again, to have a mother he can come to who will comfort him and help him with his problems. We are all sinners, and when we feel conscious of our sins and we see clearly how much right God has to reject us, when we realize our weakness and our inability to repent, when we find ourselves surrounded by temptation and assailed by evil desires, then we need our Lady's maternal love to protect, defend, and console us; we need to listen to her affectionate and encouraging words, which keep us free from all danger. When we feel alone and helpless, surrounded and weighed down by our sins, like lost children in a huge unknown city, with our hearts cold and anguished, paralyzed by loneliness, then it is she who with her tenderness restores our peace and confidence, and we know we are protected, sheltered, and defended; only then do we begin to feel that everything will work out well in spite of everything, be-

⁵ *The Way*, no. 495.
⁶ *The Way*, no. 513.

cause she loves us and will not abandon us, because we are her children.

Our Lord promised his disciples that he would not leave them orphans (Jn 14:18); he left them the Virgin as their mother. A mother is she who gives to the home a note of femininity and warmth; it is she who makes the home a place of refuge and care; she looks after our comfort and keeps everything moving harmoniously. She is the bond of union, she is the heart of the house. Protestantism gives the appearance of being cold and disunified, and it is probably because it is a home that has no mother: our Lady is absent from it, and it is weakly held together.

Above all else, our Lady has shown us, by her example, the way, the manner, of living in union with Jesus Christ. Both in her ordinary and discreet life as well as at those extraordinary moments she has left us a very simple lesson: easy to grasp and easy to imitate. She has shown us that in the world, in the home, in the ordinary daily tasks, in the duty of each moment, it is possible to achieve perfection and the very highest degree of sanctity; she has revealed to us the mystery of vocation, and how those who know that mystery find a deep meaning in life and know how to make little things great, common things heroic, ordinary things extraordinary. "It is to be hoped," wrote Pope Pius XII, "that everyone who meditates on the glorious example of Mary will become more and more convinced of the value of human life if it is devoted entirely to carrying out the will of the heavenly Father and the good of one's neighbor." Self-surrender to each one's particular vocation according to the will of the Father: that is what gives value to life.[7]

It should be to us a constant source of joy to know that we are children of such a Mother. In giving her to us as our Mother. God gave us such a proof of love that only our habitual laziness and reluctance to think explain why we do not thank him as we should. Undoubtedly "we have an advocate with the Father, Jesus Christ the just" (1 Jn 2:1), but God in his kindness, who knows our misery so well, has also given us

[7] See *Christ Is Passing By*, nos. 9, 91, 110, 116, and others.

a Mother to intercede for us. It is she, the *Virgo fidelis*, who helps us to understand the only thing necessary: faithfulness in the complete fulfillment of our vocation in life.